CW00862916

Let's Practise

Be a Better Musician

Susan Whykes

authorHOUSE®

AuthorHouse™ UK Ltd.
500 Avebury Boulevard
Central Milton Keynes, MK9 2BE
www.authorhouse.co.uk
Phone: 08001974150

First published by AuthorHouse 6/19/2009

ISBN: 978-1-4389-2933-0 (sc)

Printed in the United States of America
Bloomington, Indiana

This book is printed on acid-free paper.

Acknowledgements

I am thankful to all my pupils, past, present and future, who have helped form the background for this book and for patiently trying out the ideas and games. A special mention goes to Mandy who helped me formulate some of the ideas on polishing up pieces ready for performance and on performance anxiety.

I am so very grateful for the help and support from my family who have encouraged me every step of the way. They have been dragged in to read every page of this tome, pumped for ideas and information and have tested out some of the games on their own pupils. Without them this book would never have made it to the publisher.

A special thanks goes to my daughter Anne, who diligently and painstakingly proofread for me.

Thank you, one and all.

Contents

Part 1: Let's Practise 1

Part 2: Let's Perform 123

A practice a day keeps
the teacher at bay.

Part 1

Let's Practise

Introduction

Building Skyscrapers

Are you practising to the best of your ability? Are you making the most of that time you spend when it is just you, your instrument and your music? All the successful musicians in the world have developed practice habits that have lifted them from the level of the also-rans to the top of their profession.

Let's Practise (Part One) is here to help raise the standard of your work. With the help of the ideas in this book you can create a practice routine that works for you. You can find the tools to do your work thoroughly and efficiently. You can challenge yourself through the games, so that you find out how well you actually know your pieces without discovering that at the next lesson.

Using this book will help you build a musical skyscraper with firm foundations that will weather any storm. It will help you pay attention to the essential ingredients that make for effective practice.

Let's Perform (Part Two) has ideas to help you with your emotional and physical preparation for the up-and-coming concert or exam. It doesn't matter what musical instrument you play. This book is written for students of any musical discipline to help you prepare to the best of your ability whether you are sharing your music through exams, end of term concerts or perhaps just a lesson.

This book is not a cure-all. It won't help at all if it simply sits on the shelf unread! Open its pages and you will discover some mighty tools to help you so read on through this book to discover some ways of improving your practice so that you spend your time wisely and make obvious improvements.

A Word To Pupils

Learning to play a musical instrument is one of the most fulfilling and satisfying talents that you could have. Yet sometimes you have to put up with your friends poking fun at you because you have to leave a school class so that you can go to your music lesson, or because you have to do your practice before you can go out to play. So, learning a musical instrument means that you are developing a strong character.

Everyone is born with some form of musical 'intelligence', which means that a part of our brain is specially developed for hearing musical sounds. There is a big debate about whether children are influenced by their background or simply born with a talent, but even Mozart, one of the world's most talented youngsters, had to practise. Wolfgang Amadeus Mozart could compose by the age of five and by thirteen had written symphonies, operettas, sonatas and concertos, could play the harpsichord, violin and organ and was one of the better billiards players in Europe. Was he an extraordinary and special child or was he very hardworking with an enthusiastic father? Whatever the answer, it is true to say that all children have an amazing capacity to learn, with the ability to see, hear, feel and understand. You will learn to use all these senses to help you pay attention to your practice and then play your instrument in a relaxed and confident style.

A Word About Parents

Even if you are the only person in your family that plays a musical instrument, your parents will be able to help you with your music, by listening and by working with you through this book and by looking through your practice notebook to see what needs to be done before the next lesson. They can play some of the games with you, and reward you for a job well done.

A Word About Teachers

Your teacher has to do two jobs in your lesson: the first one is to teach you new things, and the other is to comment on your work. In every lesson your teacher will want to teach you something new, but they can only do that if you have practised the work that was set for you. Unless there is a good reason why you have not practised at home, you should expect that your teacher would not be pleased with you.

However, even with the best teacher in the world, sometimes we get stuck with our practice.

This book is for you!

Read on …and happy practising!

Chapter 1

Practising?

"WHY should I practise?"

Perhaps you have a half-hour lesson once a week, a mere thirty minutes in seven days. This means that for the vast, vast majority of your time you are *not* having a lesson and you are responsible for your own music making. Although there may be many important things learnt in a lesson, the great improvements are made *between* lessons.

So, you can see, the reason why teachers ask us to practise is because this is the way we make progress; we solve problems, develop our musical ability and think about the music. Owing to the variety of different things that happen in a piece of music and the rhythmic beat of the music pushing us onwards, learning to play an instrument is often characterised by a scrabbling, hope-for-the-best, out-of-control sort of approach. So we need to have a system that allows us to work with our ears, fingers and intellect together in unison. Practice time is when we are responsible for improving and developing. No one else can do it for us.

It is the **quality** of practice that is important, and not the **quantity.** If you have forgotten to practise all week and try to cram in all your work just before you go for your lesson you may 'get away with it' by playing your pieces well enough. But it is yourself you have cheated. Have you really improved? Can you play that really horrible bar perfectly every time, or did it just about work in the lesson?

Playing through your pieces is not the same as practising.

Here are some good reasons to practise:

- You have an exam or a concert to play for.
- You have been told to learn something for next lesson by your teacher and you are scared of her/him.
- You like to be able to tick off the boxes in your practice diary to show that you have done it.
- You like the challenge of training yourself, just like a footballer will practise his skills all the time.
- You like your teacher and you want to please her/him.
- Your parents encourage, or nag, you to do some work.
- You enjoy the pieces.
- You have been bribed to practise with more pocket money.

Have you ever forgotten to do your practice and had to think up an excuse to stop you getting into trouble with your teacher? I asked some teachers what excuses they had heard and here are some of the things they said:

- "The cat ate the music."
- "My baby sister hid my flute."
- "It rained all day on Saturday."
- "I've lost my keyboard."
- "My street was invaded by aliens."
- "I sprained my toe."
- "I won't practice because I don't like my instrument."
- "I don't like the piano; I wanted to play the flute instead."
- "I can't be bothered."
- "I like playing, but I hate practising."
- "I like my lessons, but I am too busy to do any practice."
- "I can't practise because I have to go to after-school clubs or a child-minder every day."
- "No-one at home plays music, so I can't get any help."

Let's look at some **frequently asked questions** concerning practising:

"WHAT shall I practise?"

You need to know clearly what to practise. If you could put the information into your 'mind's eye' you would remember it better. Well, a way of doing it is for **you** to write what needs to be done for the week into your notebook, rather than letting your teacher do it for you. It may take a bit more time if you do the writing, but you will remember it better.

"WHERE should I practise?"

Teachers always say that you should make a place available that is well lit, warm enough, with plenty of room and which is free from distractions like TVs, sisters and mobile phones.

However, most of us don't like feeling that we are all on our own when we practise. We like to be with our family, playing perhaps in the living room or in the hall. Wherever you practise, leave the instrument out (safely) or the piano lid invitingly open so that you can play whenever you feel like it. (Don't try this, though, when everyone is watching 'Dr Who'. You won't be at all popular!)

If you can't practise at home, can you practise at school, or at a friend's house? It is worth asking about this. Childminders have a busy life, but if you have to go to one after school, ask nicely if you can play your instrument there.

If you are playing an instrument, you will need a music stand. It is all right to prop the music on a mantelpiece, but laying music on the bed and bending over it to play it is definitely bad for you and may result in poor standing or sitting postures, headaches and sloppy fingering.

"WHEN should I practise?"

If possible, do it at the same time every day, like just after breakfast or when you get in from school. You need to make this a habit that you can stick to. It could be done as part of your homework routine.

A break away from intensive homework and playing your instrument actually makes you more mentally alert, and may be more fun.

However, I know many pupils who do all their homework and then put off doing some practice because they are too tired. This is fine once or twice, but if it happens every night, then you need to think again about when in your day you can fit in a few minutes' practice.

"HOW LONG should I practise for?"

As you are going to discover in this book, there is no proper answer to this question. Parents and teachers often tell us that we should practise for thirty minutes, every day. We are told that if we practise for thirty minutes every day, we will make impressive progress, whereas, if we only do five minutes just before our lesson, then we do not deserve to make any progress. Well, it might be good for your character, but there are better ways of working than being forced to spend half an hour with your music, especially if you don't know how to use the time. A little child might be able to do all their work in five minutes, but more advanced pupils may have scales and difficult pieces to work on; but **the rule** is that once you have focussed on the section you have been set, there is no need to do more at that time (unless you want to).

Most students want to get away with as little practice as possible! You want to be ready for your next lesson, but you have such little time to devote to practise. However, if you take notice of the practice tips in this book, you will not be focussed on *how long* you will need to practise for, but *how* and *what* you are practising.

Most people can only *really* concentrate for five to ten minutes at a go, but what your teacher wants you to do is not to watch the clock and just do your set time but rather, learn to work efficiently and effectively. You'll become so clever at practising that you can earn yourself some time off! Read the chapter called Building a Skyscraper for ideas on how to practise efficiently.

"HOW MANY TIMES should I practise?"

In an ideal world you should practise every day. This can be difficult but you do need to do it as often as possible. Practice is best done little and often, every day if possible, but should be done at least four times a week if you are to make any progress.

"All my parents do is nag me about my practice."

"If I don't do it then I have to do double the next time, and it feels like a punishment."

Well, let's look at this a bit. It is often difficult to practise, and despite all my best efforts in this book, it will sometimes be a struggle. Your parents are paying good money for you to learn music, so they have a right to nag you if they feel that you should be working harder. In this book you are going to learn how to shape your practice task so that it is do-able and manageable. Perhaps you will feel better about doing it then. You might like to look at how to plan your practice sessions in chapter 13.

"Why should I practise?"

The problem is you won't really improve if you don't try to do a little work every day. If you don't improve, then you just stay at the same level doing the same things and then you will get bored. Or your teacher may give you new things to do and you don't truthfully understand them, so you feel lost and confused, and then you feel even less inclined to practise.

Bite the bullet, and do a bit of work. Even five minutes every day will move you on from where you are now. Try to do it at the same time every day…and **reward** yourself for doing it. How about giving yourself a treat for doing five minutes every day for five days… like the next day off! You definitely need to use the **weekly planner** or the **weekly planner plus rewards day.**

"No-one at home plays an instrument, so I can't get any help."

This is a problem, I agree. However, it isn't a proper excuse for not doing any work at home. Even just playing through your pieces is better than doing no work at all, but how about playing through your pieces and then asking someone to listen to you? Tell them what you have been focussing on, like dynamics or slurs. Explain what should be happening when you play and then get them to put their hand up when they hear it as you perform your music. This way you will get some help without it just being "Very nice, dear. Now, supper's ready!"

"I've run out of excuses but I still won't practise!"

> 'Images received from the unconscious can give you important information about yourself and advise on the most suitable course of action.'
>
> (Rachel Charles, *Your Mind's Eye*, 2000)

What this means is that if you sit down quietly and let your practice come into your mind, what is it like? Is it black and dense? Is it like a brick wall? Is it awkward and spiky? Or is it so high you can't see over the top?

You could draw it if you wanted to. Is there a word or a phrase that you would give to your picture as a title? Read it and feel it.

Now do the task again, but this time imagine you have succeeded in doing your practice. How do you feel now? Happy, relieved, excited? Can you draw this picture and give this one a title?

How do you feel about tackling the task now? Do you feel you can go and get on, or is there something still holding you back?

If you still don't feel like doing it, then perhaps it is because the task is too daunting, and you don't see how to get on top of it. In other words it is not the music that is the problem, but how to do it; the *process* of doing it has no appeal. Well, we are going to look at the process in detail in the following chapters.

"HOW should I practise?"

Always really listen constructively when you practise, not just hearing yourself play, but really going about it thoughtfully and being determined to make the most of your practice time. See chapters 2, 3 and 4 for information on careful practising.

> There is a solution to every problem.

"Practice is so boring; just doing the same old thing every day."

There is, unfortunately, a certain amount of repetition about practice that we all hate, but every good athlete, footballer, or racing car driver has to practise their skill to get better, or to stay at the top; every top quality footballer, tennis player or racing driver has spent many, many hours honing and perfecting their skills. So we are up there with the best; but practice, to be done well, has to be **thoughtful**. It is no good just racing through a bit at break-neck speed, just to get it over with.

"I hate practising scales. I don't mind playing my pieces, but scales are so boring. Why do I have to do them?"

You need to practise playing scales and technical exercises because they help you develop good breathing, tonguing and so on. Without a good technique you won't be able to improve and won't be able to play fun pieces well enough. Challenge yourself with the ideas in chapter 10 about scales.

"Does practice make perfect?"

Well, if I wanted to be awkward, I could argue about what 'perfect' really means. Does playing musically and with fluency mean that the music has to be absolutely without errors of any kind? It would be excellent if you could get your music to that standard. You certainly should be aiming to achieve this level of perfection. So, if you are prepared to practise then you will get the great results you deserve.

"My teacher says I don't practise properly, but I don't know what he means. I play through my pieces every day, so what am I doing wrong?"

Sometimes, we teachers can BE the problem.

We play the piece to you, with good posture, good tone, nice dynamics, appropriate tempo, fluently and without comments.

We mean well; we are trying to inspire you and hope that you will aspire to play the piece like that yourself. BUT…

You then go home and try to play the piece like that! You do exactly what we have asked of you, all at once, just like that. You spend half an hour a day, every day, doing it just like that. You play through as well as you can, get stuck at the hard bits and then valiantly carry on, only to get the comment at the next lesson, "Didn't you do any work on this piece at all?"

"But I played the piece reasonably well, didn't I? My parents thought I was doing quite well, and they were pleased I was working so hard."

The problem is that your teacher has built up your expectations of how the music should go, without mentioning all the ways of working on the piece. They played it through to you and then told you to learn the music. If they don't give you the tools to do it, then they only have themselves to blame for having a frustrated and disenchanted pupil!

Chapter 2

Learning a New Piece

You are going to learn how to practise a new piece of music.

However, I am going to start with a complicated bit first.

Did you know you have **two brains**?

"Two Brains?"

You learn through:

- Sight, sound and touch.
- Using your listening, kinaesthetic (learning by physically doing) and intellectual skills.
- Involving your emotions, muscles, mind and imagination.
- Example, demonstration, and imitation.
- Exploration, discovery and creativity.
- Practising, repeating and remembering.
- Using your right brain and your left brain.

You could try asking yourself these questions to see which side of your brain you use:

1. Do you know what sound you are aiming for? - left brain
2. Do you know what it should feel like? - right brain
3. Are you sensitive to what it feels like as you play? - right brain

4. Can you read every note and symbol on the written page? - left brain
5. Can you see the musical and rhythmic shapes both with your eyes and in your mind? - right brain

Right Brain:

Your right brain learns by using the whole body (holistic), by somehow being able to know something without consciously understanding it (intuitive) and by using its imagination. Your right brain sees and understands melody and rhythm, and thinks things like "let's just play this through to see how it goes." Learning is somewhat sub-conscious. Unfortunately, a lot of practice is rather like this. The inattentive but enjoyable work done at home often does not stand up to the slight pressure put on it when playing it to your teacher. There are cries of "it went better at home" because it has not had the discipline of the logical left brain. It controls the LEFT side of your body.

Left Brain:

Your left brain, on the other hand, learns step by step, methodically, analytically, intellectually and consciously. This is what generally happens in lessons. "First you do this, and then you do that." In order to connect with this second by second perfection of the process in your practice sessions, you need to work by slow degrees, methodically, breaking the tasks down into bite-sized pieces and playing at a secure and slow speed. It can't be rushed and may seem boring and slow, but you will be pleased with the results if you take it carefully. It controls the RIGHT side of your body.

A great deal of this book will focus on the left brain style of learning because you are going to use a thoughtful, analytical, intellectual and conscious approach to your practice.

Using your skills:

Not everybody learns the same way. Some pupils will avidly read every note and enjoy the sensation of touch and sound, and yet have a very poor idea of what it is they have just played. Others will hear the teacher demonstrate the music to them, and then copy it by ear, feeling the way the music rises and falls, whilst others will play by looking for the patterns and shapes that the music makes on the written page.

But, to be a good learner, you need to involve all these skills.

"But I don't know what my teacher means!"

Sometimes music teachers are guilty of being lazy about instructions concerning your practice. They say things like "learn this bit," and "do some work on this tricky bit," or "just polish this piece," without realising that, whilst they may understand what they mean by this, the pupil may not have a clue about what they are hoping they will do!

Dictionary of sloppy terms:

- **Learn:**

What does 'learn' mean? Is it that I can play the piece through perfectly, at the right tempo and with no breakdowns? Is it when I can play it through reasonably well, with a few stumbles? Hands separately, or hands together? Is it to be memorised? Does it have to be of a high standard all the way through?

- **Tidy Up (or Polish it up):**

Help! What exactly does this mean? I know how to tidy up my bedroom (by shoving everything under the bed, so that the room looks clear) but how do I tidy up a piece? Yes there is a bit of a fluffy moment getting from one bar to the next where I have to play right and left hands together, but how am I supposed to get that any better? I know it says *rallentando* at the end of the page, but how slow is slow?

- **Speed it up:**

Well, at least this is easy. I just make my fingers go faster. This is fine, but there is a bar or two that I can't really play very well, but that's OK because I will just zoom up to that bit, go cautiously through there and then go fast again. Do I need to keep taking care of the fingering and the notes, or shall I just go fast and hope for the best?

- **Be aware of dynamics:**

Traditionally, dynamics take up a lot of lesson time. It seems as if the teacher waits until the piece is sufficiently ready for something new to happen. The pupil has overlooked them, and the teacher has to be there to help the pupil make the music more interesting.

Sloppy Directions:

Two things will happen because of sloppy directions: firstly, you will try to do something on the work set, after all you don't want to have your teacher on your back about lack of work but secondly, you don't want to do any more practice than you have to!

So you will probably take 'learn' to mean 'be able to play most of the notes from the beginning to somewhere near the end.' It won't matter if you have to stop now and again. You won't bother with such things as fingering, counting and good tone for after all, isn't that what 'polish the piece' means?

So you turn up to your next lesson. At first all is going well. You are stumbling through the piece, making some sort of progress, but your teacher has that look on his face that says, "have you done any work on this piece at all?"

It's not fair! You tried to 'learn' the piece, and you gave up your valuable time to do it, and now you are being given a hard time!

Really it isn't your fault: the problem lies with the words that the teacher used. These words mean something to your teacher because they have worked with *their* teacher and found out, probably the hard way, what is required.

So, for the moment, this book will try and help you to see what was meant, and how to go about the task of preparing your work for the next lesson.

Practising is the chore that has to be done if you want to improve your playing but we are all human, and we have other things in our lives that we want to do as well as make progress on our instruments. We want a system that allows us to achieve as much as possible in as little time as possible.

Chapter 3

Begin To Build A Skyscraper

To build a musical skyscraper with firm foundations you will need to know the **jobs** to be done, the **tools** you need to have so that you can work efficiently and **how long** this will take you.

You will need to:

- Wake up your brain and fingers ready for practice.
- Divide up the music into manageable chunks before you start your practice.
- Learn the notes, concentrating on the notes and fingering as well as counting the beats.
- Focus on details in the piece, thinking carefully about the rhythm, slurs, the speed of the fast quavers etc.
- Tackle any tricky bits. Often these tigers leap out at you when the music stops doing one pattern and changes direction.
- Test out your practice to see if you really know your notes by playing some games.

Because all these points need explaining, so that you understand how to develop and improve your practice, there is a chapter on each topic.

Let's start from the beginning.

Some Physical Warm-ups.

The human brain has, for the purposes of this book, two sides, and we are utilising these in our learning tasks. However, to gain mastery over the learning process, we need to cross over these two sides, or 'centre' ourselves. When we are centred, we are focussed, able to express our emotions and keep our fears at bay. If we are uncentred, we suffer irrational fears, fight-or-flight responses or an inability to feel or express emotions. (Doesn't this sound like us when we are in the throes of performance anxiety?)

Research done by Educational Kinesiologists has resulted in some interesting and rewarding self-help exercises to develop learning through movement. The 'Brain Gym' movements should help you to experience these vitalising effects in both your daily activities and in these specific learning tasks.

None of the following exercises should give you any discomfort. You should never move in a way that feels unnatural or uncomfortable, and certainly never forced. To see these exercises demonstrated go to **www.youtube.com/watch?v=18f_cgeydGo**

Cross Crawl:

Let's get both sides of the brain working by doing a 'cross crawl'. This is like walking in place but you move one arm and the opposite leg, and then the other arm and its opposite leg.

> Put your right hand behind your back and reach down. Lift your left foot up behind you. Touch your left ankle with your right fingers. Then change over and touch your left fingers to your right ankle.
>
> Do this for about one minute or twenty times.
>
> An alternative is to try to touch your right elbow onto your left knee, and then your left elbow to your right knee.
>
> You will feel very co-ordinated after this exercise.

Neck Roll:

This exercise relaxes the neck and releases tensions. If you do this before you start work you will see more clearly and hear more acutely.

Allow your head to roll slowly from side to side as though it were a heavy ball, breathing deeply as you do this. Do not let your chin pass either side of your collarbone.

If you find any tight spots or tension, hold the head in that position, breathing deeply until your neck releases.

Do neck rolls with your eyes open and with your eyes closed too.

Finish your relaxation by imagining a warm waterfall flowing down the back of your neck.

Belly Breathing:

First you need to breathe in through your nose and then let the air out in one long out-breath through the lips, pursed as if you are keeping a feather in the air.

Now breathe in to a count of three, hold your breath for three, breathe out for three and hold for three. If you take longer to breathe out than in, you get a better sense of relaxation.

Thinking Cap:

Get your memory working and your thinking skills going with the 'thinking cap'. In this activity you use your thumbs and index fingers to pull your ears gently back and unroll them. Begin at the top of the ear and gently massage down and around the curve and ending at the bottom lobe.

Energy Points:

Another tip for helping your thinking is to gently touch the energy points above each eye with the fingertips of each hand. The points are on the little bumps halfway between the hairline and the eyebrows. This activates the brain to perform well and has an effect on the adrenalin flow round the body. People sometimes rub or hold their foreheads when they are thinking or remembering something.

Also, have a **glass of water** to energise your brain. Ask your teacher about some specific physical warm-ups you can do at your standard of playing. For example, flute players can pout their lips, blow kisses into the air, and twitch their upper lips as a rabbit might do. Pianists can tap with one finger in turn whilst keeping all the other four digits resting on the tabletop.

Now you are ready to begin work.

Chapter 4

Chunks

You look at a new piece and there are notes all over the place. What an intimidating task! How is all this information to be sorted out? In fact the job may be so daunting that you don't want to try out the new piece, and just stick at playing music you already know, or give up practising altogether.

Don't you think that new pieces should come with a tool-kit and instructions on how to do it? This is exactly what we have got. These tools and instructions can be used on any new piece, removing the fear about how you are going to manage and giving you a feeling that you have everything under control.

Note well: this tool-kit will not necessarily give you a piece fit to be performed in one week, but will build up your understanding and fluency so that the piece will stand up to being performed later on.

Maybe your teacher made a note in your practice diary for this week's work that went something like this:

> Learn F major two octaves
> Learn the first page of the Mozart *Andante in C*
> Tidy up Study 17

Your teacher is probably expecting you to do this in seven days ready for your next lesson.

Your teacher's list is fine, and you can see what needs to be done, but these jobs are too big in themselves and can't be done all at once.

In order to be able to achieve the goal of doing all your work in as short a time as possible, but still do it thoroughly, methodically and thoughtfully, the tasks your teacher set need to be planned out.

To 'tidy up' your study have a look at the chapter on 'Getting Your Piece Right' and try the Rollette game every day to work this music up to a higher standard.

If you have any theory to do, you can also split that into manageable chunks and do some every day along with your practice.

You are going to change the look of the list to make the big jobs into smaller ones. Say there are twenty-four bars on page one of the Mozart *Andante in C*, and there are six more days before the next lesson. This means we can create six groups of four bars each and have either one day off or a day for revision.

Now instead of 'Learn the Mozart *Andante in C*' you could try this:

> Day 1   Learn bars 1 - 4
> Day 2   Learn bars 5 - 8
> Day 3   Learn bars 9 - 12
> Day 4   Learn bars 13 - 16
> Day 5   Learn bars 17 - 20
> Day 6   Learn bars 21 - 24
> Day 7   Revision day

Label each section of your Mozart: bars 1 - 4 section a, 5 - 8 section b, 9 - 12 section c, etc.

The way the music is divided is up to you, but the smaller the number of bars in a section the more sections you will have, and conversely, the greater the number of bars the more work you will have to do to complete a 'floor'. Perhaps you should read on to the next step before finally deciding how many bars you want to work with at a time.

You are going to work on the tasks in each floor of your skyscraper. You take the section you labelled 'a', for example, and begin work at the first floor doing all the tasks in the list below. Once you have completed the first floor, you can move on to the second floor.

When you had a look at the piece of music in your lesson you probably had no idea about the music, but perhaps by the next lesson you will have got section 'a' up to floor 4. So you will have made progress with your piece. Well done!

However, before you even break your music down into manageable chunks look at it carefully.

Most music breaks down into patterns and chunks of ideas that repeat themselves. If you look through the piece in detail, you will be surprised at how many things you know about the music even before you start work on it.

Have a look through and notice:

- All the times sections **repeat** themselves. If the patterns re-occur, you only have to do one bit of work instead of two. This is a great offer: two for the price of one!
- All the times that the **rhythms/motifs** are the same.
- The notes affected by the **key signature.**
- Patterns of **scales/arpeggios/chromatics.**
- Passages that are **similar** to ones you've done in another piece.

Notice too:

- All the sections where you know you can play well.
- All the really easy bits.

You could make your music look pretty if you highlight all the matching bars in one colour, patterns in a different colour, rhythms in another and so on.

By the time you have noticed all these bits, there won't be much left to actually learn!

Build a skyscraper:

Imagine a skyscraper with eight floors, (eleven for pianists). Each floor has a different task and to get to the top of the building you need to have worked through each task.

Have a look at the floors:

For instrumentalists:

	Find the bar or section you are going to target, then:
Floor 1	Count out loud and clap the rhythm of the notes.
Floor 2	Finger and say the note names but without blowing or bowing them.
Floor 3	Play the notes with no errors. (Gaps are allowed while working out the next note.)
Floor 4	Play the notes slowly, but count in your head or tap with your foot.
Floor 5	Play the notes with a metronome going slowly, thus not being allowed to stop and think if you get stuck.
Floor 6	Play the notes from memory but you can stop and think about what comes next.
Floor 7	Play the notes from memory but with the metronome going slowly, so now there is no time to stop and think.
Floor 8	Play the notes from memory with a metronome at three-quarters of the required tempo.

For pianists:

Find the bar or section you are going to target, then:

Floor 1　　Count out loud and clap the rhythm of the notes.

Floor 2　　Play through the right hand, saying the letter names.

Floor 3　　Play through the left hand, saying the letter names.

Floor 4　　Play slowly hands together, saying the letter names.

Floor 5　　Play right hand from memory, first with the piano lid shut and then on the piano keys.

Floor 6　　Play left hand from memory, first with the piano lid shut and then on the piano keys.

Floor 7　　Play hands together from memory but you are allowed to stop and think.

Floor 8　　Play right hand from memory with a metronome set at a slow speed. There are no thinking time gaps allowed.

Floor 9　　Play left hand played from memory with a metronome going slowly. There are no thinking time gaps allowed.

Floor 10　　Play hands together from memory with a metronome still going slowly.

Floor 11　　Play hands together from memory with a metronome at three-quarters of the required tempo.

The lists look rather daunting, but become a straightforward and efficient way of working once you have got the hang of them. Just stick at it and you will reap the rewards.

It is worth remembering that it is often where the <u>patterns alter</u> or <u>change direction</u> that you are likely to trip up, so pay special attention to these areas to develop your fluency here.

Some definitions:

- **Play** means to play through the notes once from beginning to end without any mistakes or incorrect things like fingerings. Split notes and notes that don't come out or sound clear count as mistakes.
- **Play hands separately with and without sound:** so that your left brain (that operates your right body) and your right brain (that operates your left body) can get disentangled and get clear on what they are supposed to be doing. You can even do this on a woodwind instrument to check your fingering! Do you know what your left hand is doing when your right hand is busy fingering the lower notes?
- **Playing hands together with and without sound:** slowly, put the two parts back together again, and repeat the process of playing it on the piano lid before trying it out loud. Imagine it as you play it to get the feel of the correct way of playing that section. *Remember you are allowed to take as long as you like to play from one note to the other.* The challenge is to play it right, not to see how fast you can go! If it takes you sixteen seconds to go from note one to note two…well it may not flow well yet, but the important thing is to get it correct.
- **From memory** simply means to play the notes without looking at the music. Turn the book over but don't shut your eyes.
- **Look and see** what you are doing.
  If you are a flute player, turn your flute as if it were a recorder or rest it on your shoulder and look at your fingers to see what they have to do to play those notes before you try and play them out loud.
  If you are a pianist, then look at the keys you are using. Just like learning spellings, you need to SEE the individual letters that make up your word; you need to SEE what you are using to make your music.
  You are still using the **Play** rules though, so you can still take as long as you need between notes.
- With a Metronome, however, means that those nice gaps between notes when you were thinking about them have now

gone. Make sure that the metronome speed is slow enough for you to play your notes at a sensible pace, but you have to play all the right notes at the right time. You will need to have the speed **nice and slow**, but also be aware of the rhythm of the notes you are using so that you get that correct too.

You don't always need to start at the beginning of the piece and battle your way to the end. When you are practising, you can think of music as if it were a **jigsaw puzzle**. You can take the music to bits and look carefully at small sections of it. Why not photocopy your music and cut it into pieces along some bar lines or into suitable short sections? You could then pick one at random and practise just that. You need to be able to play it perfectly three times before you try another bar.

In any piece of music there are bars that are quite easy and others that look tricky.

There are two ways of doing the jigsaw puzzle:

- You could work on these tricky sections first so that all the other practices will consist of learning the easy sections.
- You could do one difficult section and one easy bit in the same practice session.

See the next page for a game.

Jigsaw Puzzles:

You will need:

- Two small pots (jam jar, cups or even a couple of saucers will do).
- Your piece of music cut into small sections, e.g. a bar or a phrase.

The object of the game:

To move all the bars into pot 2.

To play:

- Put all the bars into pot 1.
- Select one at random and play it through.
- If you were successful, with NO mistakes, wobbly bits or wrong fingerings, then you can put this bar into pot 2.
- Pick another bar at random and play this.
- Every time you are successful, transfer the bar to pot 2.
- Every time you make a mistake, you have to place it back in pot 1.

If you can't get a *really* tricky bit right it can go on one side to be practised separately. See the chapter on Getting Stuck and Unstuck.

Other ways to practise are:

1. Worst bits first:

You could start with the worst bits first and get them practised before going onto something a little less scary. It certainly makes sense to do the hard task and then reward yourself by doing something easier because it is always a good idea to finish with a nice feeling. You feel more positive about your work and will be more likely to go back and practise again. There is a downside to this, however. If you have spent a week practising the difficult bit, you may have little to show your teacher the next lesson.

2.   Half and half:

You might like to do half and half practice. In this method, you choose one tricky part and one easy passage to practise. This way you are not always struggling with the hard bits but get a few minutes with something easier in the same practice session. This way you do have something more to show to the teacher, but it is a matter of choice.

Instrumentalists who are more advanced may find the skyscraper levels too easy. So you will need to build the Eiffel Tower!

The Eiffel Tower Method:

Floor 1	Count and clap the rhythm from the first beat of the first bar to the first beat of the next one to work out where all the notes fit into the bar.
Floor 2	Set the kitchen timer or use the timer on your mobile phone for five minutes. Think first. Try to imagine which fingers play which notes before you play it out loud. Finger the notes and say out loud the note names and then play them until the timer goes ping.
Floor 3	Use a distorted rhythm, or several styles of distorted rhythm to practise the notes as well as a straight rhythm. There is an example at **www.youtube.com/ watch?v=18f_cgeydGo** on distorted rhythms.
Floor 4	Put the timer back on and do an easy bit over and over for the next five minutes. When the five minutes is up, stop that task.
Floor 5	Play something else completely or go back to the difficult section again and do another five minutes.

Be careful about the use of the timer. It is not about the *amount* of time you spend, but the *quality* of the concentration you give during that time.

If you don't get it right, then you don't pass that floor and if you don't pass that floor you cannot move on to the next one.

You won't get hit by lightning, or fall into the centre of the earth! Just start again and work through the list from the top.

There are some things to remember though:

- There may be a problem with dividing up your music into the same-sized chunks, because not all bars are going to be as easy as each other. You may find that a couple of bars are really difficult, whereas there may be a group of six bars that are really quite straightforward. So you may have to revise the way you divide up your music, but once you have got the idea of splitting up your jobs into manageable chunks you will make good progress. You might get the groupings terribly wrong to begin with, but you will soon get the hang of it.

- Always listen carefully and critically to what you do. If you don't listen carefully then you won't really know if you are improving or not.

- Revising your work once a week may not be enough. You may find that you actually need to revise yesterday's work at the end of today's practice. You will need to allow a few minutes for this, if this is the way you like to work.

- Practise until you have finished your tasks for the day and not to a time limit. In the example earlier there are three tasks to be done: a section of Mozart, a task from the Rollette game for your study and a theory exercise. You should keep working until you have completed all of the tasks. Once you have finished you can stop. Practice done! However, if you find that even after an hour you really feel you haven't made progress, then perhaps either the dividing up was too big, and you need to reduce the amount of work you set for each day, or the task is too difficult, in which case you will need to discuss it with your teacher.

"Why do I have to stop playing out loud?"

Did you notice, in the middle floors of your skyscraper, that you were asked to play without sound, either by shutting the lid of the piano or without blowing or bowing? This is where your two brains have come in to help you play. You are using all those kinaesthetic and intellectual skills that we learnt about at the beginning of the book. By going over the task without hearing it you have to visualise the way the music goes. It makes you aware of what your right and left hands are doing, and where the rests, fingerings, sharps and rhythm go. This may seem very difficult, but it can help to clarify fingering, notes, rhythm, key signatures, etc. If you can get your music into your mind like this, it will stay with you for much longer.

> 'Think ten times. Play once.'
>
> Chopin (a very famous pianist)

Are there any other techniques I need to know?"

To become a great musician there are other ways you can learn:

Singing while playing unites your left and right brain and helps you learn more quickly. Sing with a feeling of warmth deep within you, and slowly with musical expression. Give the first beat of the bar more weight than the others, and all of the skills you use will be able to work together at a very deep level: the left (step-by-step, counting, thinking) and right (holistic, pulse, rhythm, pitch) sides of your brain will find ways of linking together to teach the body exactly where to move and where to relax, and the intellect stays clear and uncluttered.

Moving to the beat is another excellent way to learn about pulse and beat. Physical movement also helps you to internalise musical elements such as rhythm, pitch and phrase length. If your whole body is involved in learning these musical ideas then you can feel how they go and what they mean.

Once you can experience these ideas then you will be able to express them more securely. So:

- Step the rhythm or the pulse whilst clapping the rhythm.
- Move your hands or even your whole body to show how the pitch rises and falls.

Listening to a recording of your piece may help you learn how it goes. There is a danger that you will try to play it at the speed that you hear it at far too early, but there is some value in hearing how your piece should go. Certainly we learn as much by listening to things as we do by looking. If you can follow the score and learn the rhythm or hear the dynamics then this will all help you to understand the music better. If the recording is slow enough then it can be fun to play along too. Just be careful of trying to play your music up to this final performance speed without working on it by building up your skyscraper first.

Writing out the note names that you are playing will really help too. So often we play using our eyes and fingers, which almost form a short-cut through our brain, so that we don't seem to use the actual note names when we play, but just see the notes and de-code them straight to our finger muscles. This is fine, but sometimes we make mistakes because we really are not clear about what the notes are. Can you write out the notes, either in letter names or notations from memory? If you can do this task, then you have the information clear in your head, but if you can't, then you can understand that there is probably a muddle in your head over the section you are working on. So write them out looking at the music…not just in notes on a stave, but also in letter names, and then learn them, like you'd learn your spellings at school. (You could write them out in different orders and create your own composition.)

Use distorted rhythms. This is where straight quavers can become dotted, or dotted quavers become straight, clearly accenting the strong beat of the bar. Changing the way you look at a piece of music can really upset the brain. If you have been looking at a passage with, say, thirty-two quavers in a string, the chances are that you are not really looking at the individual notes but a chunk of them, just like you would look at a word in a book. So if you change the rhythm of them, your brain and eyes are forced to see the notes in a different way. (Go to **www.youtube.com/watch?v=18f_cgeydGo** for examples.)

- You can pair up the notes and play the first one short and the second one long (dotted quaver then semiquaver) or reverse this and play the first one as the semiquaver and the second note as the dotted quaver. You can put them into triplets and play three notes as a clump, then the next three, and so on.
- You can accent the beats of the bar, or change the accent within the bar, for example, playing every third note, every fifth note or seventh note with an accent!

Teaching someone else is another great way of really getting to know what you are trying to learn. If you can explain what you are learning to another person you will find you have a better and deeper understanding of that skill or concept that you have been tackling.

Now you have some things in your tool-kit to help get your practice started, and your skyscraper built. You need to ensure that you are working at your best level, though, such as standing well enough to make your best sound, playing thoughtfully and with care.

To Summarise:

When learning a new piece:

- Use your left and right brain styles of learning to make the most of your practice sessions.
- Use your whole body when learning pulse and rhythms.
- Mark up your piece of music so you can see patterns, scales, repeats etc.
- Divide up your piece into small chunks so that you can work steadily and daily through your music.

Chapter 5

Learning the Notes

Reading the notes:

Some pupils try to get by with getting good at working with finger numbers, partly because they don't feel safe with reading notes. However, if you don't practise reading notes you won't get any better. So, if you are determined to improve, then **practise reading** notes. Do some every day. There are plenty of note-speller books around to help you. You will even find free worksheets on the Internet.

Knowing the notes:

If you know how to work the notes out but it takes you a while, then maybe you should practise reading them for a couple of weeks. Write them out, and read them out loud. You will be surprised how well you can name them after you have done a few hundred of them!

The more you do, the better you will get. You just need to find some easy music and sit down and try to play it. Take your time, work out the notes and say them out loud before you play them.

You could do it the other way round, and find the hardest music you've ever seen. Even though you are not trying to learn this piece to perform, try working out and playing the notes of a few bars slowly.

Just attempting to read these notes is useful, and will make your pieces seem much easier.

Sight-reading is actually a lot more than just naming and reading notes, but being able to name the notes is certainly part of the skill. Indeed, if you can't name the notes you will find that one day you will grind to a halt because you can't work them out. A considerable amount of time in a lesson can be spent simply correcting notes caused by poor, insecure or lazy music reading.

"I don't need to read the notes because I play my music off by heart."

A lot of pupils who are poor music readers often learn their pieces off by heart and so don't spend very much time actually looking at the notes. This is fine, and even admirable, but not good for reading and will give you trouble if you have learned bits of it wrongly.

What you need to do is to keep reading the notes, even when you don't need to. It keeps you focussed on the page, so you know *where* you are in the music as well as *what* you are playing.

"How do I actually *read* the music?"

Your eyes read by making very rapid, short movements followed by longer periods of 'fixations' (which could be looking at a letter, a word or even a sentence), where the eyes stay still, during which the actual reading and processing takes place. Your eyes are generally working forwards along the text but there are also backwards movements to check what has just been read. This sequence takes place two or three times a second.

When you read music your eyes make similar movements with some interesting differences: you make more eye movements, about five or six times a second and your eyes move backwards along the notes more often than if you read text.

In fact, your eyes scan the music both along and up and down to build up an overall picture of what you are reading. You can't train your eyes to do any other movements because these have become a habit over the years you have been reading, but an understanding of how you read can help you to increase your efficiency.

"How do I do sight-reading?"

There are three basic things you are doing when you sight-read:

1. **Recognising pitch.**

   Seeing a note, knowing what it is called, and then translating this information into the appropriate set of physical movements - all of which need to be almost simultaneous.

   Beginner sight-readers should:

   - Name the notes as you finger them.
   - Say the finger numbers if you use them.

2. **Understanding rhythm.**

   You need to really understand a steady pulse before you can build a rhythm on it. You need to practise this, so next time you start a piece, count yourself in for four bars, two out loud and two internally, but loudly, in your head. Try to keep this pulse going by gently tapping a foot or bending a knee. A steady beat is absolutely vital. You need a steady beat to hang your rhythm on and to keep your music moving steadily forward.

   Beginner sight-readers should:

   - Count and clap one or two bars of music.
   - Think or sing the counts as you play them.

3. **Combining notes and rhythm while keeping a steady pulse.**

   You need to relate pulse to rhythm. You must try to maintain a steady pulse and then see how the rhythmic pattern will sit on that pulse. You will need to make sure that you know what the notes are and what the rhythm is.

"Can I learn to sight-read?"

Yes, you can. There are many books to help you learn the tricks of the trade but basically you need to:

- Concentrate for the duration of your exercise.
- Keep counting as you play. Whether you count in numbers or just keep the beat is up to you.
- You should count out loud while you are practising.
- Note the time signature. This will help you decide how the beats and accents will go. For example, if you are in 6/8 time will you find it more comfortable counting in two dotted crotchets to a bar or six quavers?
- Look carefully at the rhythm. This is the problem area for most sight-readers.
- Choose quite a slow tempo. The biggest mistake pupils make is trying to play too fast. If you go too fast you are bound to have a slip.
- Tap the pulse with your left hand, or with your foot, and tap the rhythm with your right hand. (Now reverse this if you are a pianist so that you tap the steady pulse with your right hand and tap the rhythm with your left hand.)
- Rhythm is a matter of co-ordination and the more you try the better you will get at tapping and keeping a steady beat.
- Notice the key signature. Which notes will be altered and how? Visualise how to play them on your instrument by closing your eyes and imagining how your fingers move.
- Before you play the piece read through the notes carefully. Look for patterns in the music. These could be in the melody, or a rhythm that repeats itself. These will help you as you play through the piece. Since you are only learning how to sight-read, work out the notes and say them out loud as you read along the piece.
- Look for any tricky bits and work out what happens in them by looking carefully and slowly at them.
- Visualise it in your mind - as best you can. Reading it through and remembering it will give you an idea of 'how the music goes', which is important when you are doing this on your own

at home. Remember those patterns that you spotted earlier to help shape the image you have in your mind.

- Play through, only touching the keys but not playing out loud yet. In exam situations you should try to speed-read this task, but for now you are allowed to go as slowly as you want to. Keep a steady beat, even if it is a very slow one.
- Play through again but playing out loud, giving all your attention to the notes. Play through slowly but at a steady pace, trying hard to keep the rhythms and notes going as well as possible. Don't stop to correct errors here. (If you don't feel ready to play the melody yet, try and sing it first.)
- After your play-through stop and criticise your playing and see if you can remember where your mistakes were.
- Now play it again, trying to still maintain your steady beat but correcting your mistakes.

When you do sight-reading for an exam you are not supposed to play at your first read-through. You prepare the sight-reading task as suggested before, especially the silent play-through.

You actually play out loud at your *second* attempt.

Good sight-readers will actually rehearse the next couple of notes a fraction of a second before they play or sing them. They make a mental plan before they carry out the action required. So it is a good idea to keep practising looking and reading at least one note ahead.

Over the page is a game for you. You will only need to do three or four bars of your music.

Musical Kim's Game

You will need:

- A piece of quite simple music (of which you will only need three or four bars).

- A timer (on your watch or mobile phone).

- A pencil and a piece of paper.

The object of the game:

To see how much of a piece of music you can remember.

To get as close as possible to 80 points.

To play:

- Set your timer for 30 seconds.

- You have to take in as much detail as possible of the three or four bars, until the timer goes off.

- When the timer goes off, turn the music over. Keep thinking about the music.

Now answer these questions without peeping at the music:

What is the key signature?	Score 5 points for a correct answer.
What is the time signature?	Score 5 points
What is the first note?	Score 5 points
What is the third note?	Score 5 points
Now can you:	
Clap the rhythm of the first two bars?	Score 20 points
Sing the first three bars?	Score 20 points
Play any of the music from memory?	Score 20 points

Total up your score and see how close you are to 80 points. If you scored 70 points or more then well done. You can stop here.

If you scored 60 points or more then turn the book over and see that the mistakes were, but you can stop here.

If you scored less than 50 points, turn the music back over and look carefully at it for 30 seconds and then play it through as you would for a piece of sight-reading. Then you can stop.

If you are regularly getting a high score, then it is time to only allow yourself twenty seconds instead and repeat the game. You can reuse the music now and again if you need to. Ask your teacher for some pieces to practise if you need some new material.

When you are sight-reading remember:

Always count, or at least keep a steady beat.

Never stop, or at least try to keep going forward all the time.

If you are still having problems reading the music, then practise some scales in the keys that you need for your standard, and you will begin to see the patterns and connections better, and be able to predict a bit more reliably what notes are quite likely to be in your piece.

To Summarise:

- Learn your notation by making certain you can read the notes, by knowing their names, by writing them out and saying them out loud.
- Practise your sight-reading with a steady beat, understanding the rhythm and saying the note names out loud by name to begin with.
- Get to know your scales.

Chapter 6

Getting Stuck and Unstuck

> There is no failure, only success.

"What should I do when I get stuck when I am practising?"

If you can figure out what exactly is causing a problem then you are halfway to solving it. Some pupils, when they get stuck on a tricky bit, react by practising it even harder. When that doesn't work, they try even harder. They spend ages working at it. Well, you would think this is a good idea, but really what they need to do now is to spend a few minutes discovering exactly why the part is so difficult, and then finding an answer to that problem.

Of course, some bits are genuinely hard, and you are entitled to think of them as such, but sometimes you have talked yourself into thinking of them as nasty. It starts off as a simple mistake the first time you play through a piece and then somehow you manage to mess it up the next few times you play that bit. Your brain then makes a new folder, labels it 'Tricky Bit' and saves it to your computer brain. Now, every time you come up to that spot in the music, your brain says, "Ah yes! I remember this bit. This is the bit I can't do," and Bob's your uncle, you can't do it!

If you allow the label to stay on that spot you will always find it tricky, even if, really, it isn't that hard. You find it difficult to relax when you get to that section, and it will always go wrong just because you are worrying over it.

Wouldn't it be nice if you could just relax about it and not worry when you get to that section? Well, part of the answer is *not* to worry about it so much! Don't let it take over your practice time.

Tricky bits are simply bits that you haven't found a solution to yet.

Tricky bits are like tigers.

Tigers and tricky bits are both wild and fierce and have a habit of frightening us. When tamed, they are rather cute! We are going to learn how to tame these tigerish bars.

"I had a spot marked on my music. It is a tricky bit. How will I work on it?"

That spot got there on your music because your teacher found that there was some sort of problem with this section, maybe a wrong note, or a rhythm that just doesn't improve. Ignoring that spot will not make it go away. If all you do every practice time is play that section the same old way you will not get that bit any better.

The advice here is *not* just to try harder and harder and practise and practise that spot but to stop and work out exactly what is making this passage difficult. Often the tricky bits stay unvisited and under-worked because we really don't know what is causing the problem, and therefore we cannot find a line of attack to solve it.

"Where is the tiger hiding?"

First you need to find exactly **where** the difficulty lies. There are probably one or two specific places that are hard, hidden inside some other slightly easier notes. Don't just look at about three bars and say, "this bit is difficult." Where precisely is the bit that won't work? After all, there are probably quite a few notes you can play with ease. So you need to find the actual bit that you find tricky.

Take the tricky bit to pieces and look at it carefully. You will see that even this is actually made up of some easy bits and some difficult ones. What are the easy parts of it? Make a list of the spots in the music that are OK, like the pedalling or the octave slurs, and look forward to those bits. It will make the section seem a little less uncomfortable and a bit more manageable.

"How should I tame the tiger?"

The next step is to find exactly **why** this bit is causing problems. It could be an awkward register change or a difficult group in the middle of a long string of fast semiquavers.

You need to find a variety of solutions that will help you with your problem. The more solutions you try, the more likely you are to stumble across the one that will help in this situation, although it might need a combination of responses to tame a tiger.

What are you going to do about it?

This actually is a big step towards defeating the problem. Being able to identify and explain the enemy clearly makes you better equipped to win the battle.

Your first task is to go back to your skyscraper floors:

- Remember all the levels that you have to work through. You need to go back over them and diligently work at them, slowly and thoughtfully.
- Take a **really small** section at a time. Even one or two notes at a time are plenty when dealing with tricky bits.
- Work thoughtfully, slowly and carefully.
- Try to learn the section off by heart, so that you can play it with confidence.
- Be prepared to repeat this work each day for a few days, doing the same skyscraper tasks every day.

"Are there any tricks of the trade that I can use to tame the tiger?"

There are several ways of going about this, and as a beginner you will need to try all of them. The tricks for taming tigers are **exaggerate, extend** and **repeat.**

Exaggerate:

- Count and clap the tricky bit.
- Name the notes as you finger them.
- Write out the letter names of the notes you are learning.
- Watch what you are doing by, for example, putting your flute on your shoulder and studying your fingering, or by watching your fingers on the piano keys.
- Play in the air with just your fingers without using your instrument.
- Visualise in your mind what you are trying to play.

Extend:

- If you can play that section once, then play it several times in a row, or make up a tune that uses that bit over and over.

Repeat:

- You can repeat the note. Suppose you had a group of notes such as G, A, B, D that are tigerish. Play them twice each; so then you would play GG, AA, BB, DD.

Other tricks are:

- Change the speed that you are playing at.
- Use distorted rhythms. You could play the tigerish bit in a jazzy rhythm, or in groups of threes as if they were triplets.
- Use a metronome and play slowly but steadily to avoid building in hesitations while you seek out the next note or chord. Then go to the chapter on **Fixing the Speed** to improve the tempo.
- Play **Downfall** to tame the tiger (see page 75).

Here is some advice about taming tigers:

Firstly: keeping trying! It is often quite difficult to actually spot the problem, but you won't find it if you just keep bashing away at the notes. Don't give up until you have looked carefully, thoughtfully and *slowly* at it.

Secondly: if it still doesn't respond to the skyscraper method then take a break from that bit. I know it sounds as if you are giving up on the problem, but really, sometimes your brain just needs to have a think about the problem and solve it in its own way.

It is a bit like when you have tried and tried to remember something, like a name or where you have seen someone before, and then you go to sleep, still puzzling over it. Then, in the middle of the night, you wake up and say, "of course, it was so and so!" It is the same thing with playing music. Sometimes your brain just needs a break from constant puzzling to do a little problem solving on its own. Try not to even think about that section, and leave it alone for even a couple of weeks. It will seem better next time you come to it because your subconscious brain has been working on the problem the whole time.

Thirdly: take it to your teacher. After all, practice is just that – practice. It is only there to accelerate improvements, not fix every single tricky bit. Having worked so well at home, you have got the piece as far as you can go for the moment. Well done!

However, **don't get mad!** It *is* frustrating when you are working hard and nothing seems to be improving, but nothing will get better if you are angry about it. If you need to, take a break from this section for today! Even professional musicians get frustrated and mad at themselves, but it is what you do next that turns disaster into success.

Don't keep doing the same old thing over and over. If you have spent the last week working on something and it is still rubbish, then you need to go about this section in a different way.

Don't let the tricky bit stop you practising the rest of the piece. The bit you are stuck on may be only two bars out of twenty-four, so really it isn't that much of the piece that isn't working.

Don't let the tricky bit stop you from practising altogether.
Sometimes we need to take a break from playing if all we seem to do ends up sounding horrid, but if you are really only having a bad time with your two bars, then do some other bits and pieces instead…(how about some scales?)

Do change something when you practise:

Since you are stuck anyway, you may as well change something. Just mixing things around can help ease the situation.

- If you usually practise in the morning, practise in the evening.
- If you usually do half an hour then try a few five minute bursts instead. (Or the other way round…if you do five minute chunks then try one or two longer stints.)
- Change the way you sit.
- Change the relaxation in your arms or fingers.
- Change which hand you watch.
- Change the speed…especially try it slower.
- Change…

Anything!

You see, the tricky bits aren't really tricky, they are just bits that you haven't yet found the solution for.

"Victory is mine!"

That bad bit is enjoying a temporary triumph over you at the moment. So you need to throw ALL of the tricks of the trade for taming tigers at it - not just some, but all of them. Use all of them on this bit and see how the tiger can be reduced to a cute little kitty cat. The chances are that the tricky bits will budge out of the way and never be seen again!

These tricks will be dealt with in the next chapters.

To Summarise:

- Go back over the levels in your skyscraper.
- Do a very small number of notes so that you can learn them off by heart.
- Work thoughtfully, slowly and carefully.
- Try some of the tricks of the trade to tame tigers.
- **Exaggerate** the problem area by writing it out, clapping and visualising it.
- **Extend** the problem by doing it over and over. Incorporate it into a short tune you could make up.
- **Repeat** the notes and the section several times.
- Don't get mad.
- Change something if you keep getting stuck.

Chapter 7

Fixing The Speed

"How am I supposed to know how fast to go?"

The first question many pupils ask is, "how fast does this music go?" This is not at all helpful, since the final, finished speed is something to work towards and not to be attempted until you have done lots of practice. In fact, as you get to know the piece your mind will recognise the music faster, your fingers will respond more quickly and so you will automatically play it more rapidly.

Speed, or tempo, is quite a problem. Some pieces of music use terms like *allegro* or *andante* and you are supposed to somehow feel the difference. When you are learning a new piece you will probably work through it quite slowly. There is so much information to absorb that it is simply too difficult to go fast since there is so little time between notes. If you take a piece of music marked a*ndante* and play quavers at a speed of 1 crotchet beat each second, you will be playing two notes to every beat. This means there is only half a second between notes. That is not really too bad, but consider playing *allegro*: here you will have five notes every second. This isn't too tricky when you know the piece, but is too fast when you are only reading through the music for the first time.

So, when you are beginning a new piece you can only play it at a fraction of the final speed. This is fine, don't worry about it.

Indeed the problem often lies with the fact that easy bits came before you arrived at the trickier section. You are playing along at a reasonable speed and then slam into the harder bit and have to go more slowly in order to cope with it.

That speed, therefore, was *too fast*. You need to work out how slowly you need to go so that you can play the tricky bit perfectly. This will dictate the speed of even the easy notes.

> Only play at a speed that will let you play it all perfectly.

So, when learning a new piece, **go slowly.**

"How slow is slow?"

You need to go only at a speed at which you make no mistakes. It is so tempting to play quickly through the easy bit and then slow up while you do the difficult bit, but this is no use to you at all.

You need to do a bargain with yourself. Here's the good news: if you set the metronome for a slow beat per minute and play all the notes (even the easy ones) at that speed then you only have to do half the practice time. If you think about it, it is better to spend half the amount of time playing perfectly, say fifteen minutes, rather than half an hour of fast and furious (but wrong) work.

Metronomes are useful tools for helping us to keep in time. You put the speed at a suitable tempo, and notice what that speed was. It really doesn't matter *how* slow it is. Work out which notes go with the tick and which ones fit in between. Mark it on your score too, so that you can see what is happening and when. Metronomes will only be useful if you understand which notes are to be played when you hear the beat.

"What exactly does 'slowly' mean?"

Most students don't wilfully play too fast. Your teacher played the piece to you so that you could hear the music being played and how it should sound when it is finished. Unfortunately, all you probably remember of it is how fast it went. You didn't pick up on the amazing *staccati*, or the sensuous dynamics, and possibly don't really remember the tune.

You go home and then have to try the music out yourself. Since the only thing you took on board was the speed, you have to play it like this to make it sound like what you heard. This is understandable and totally normal, after all, copying adults is the mainstay of the way in which children learn. Unfortunately, this is not really playing the piece, but pretending you are.

Ideally, the teacher should play the piece at the speed they want it to go for this week, but teachers are only human too, and they don't want to spend your lesson playing the piece to you at the speed you really should go at. So you must take responsibility for this yourself.

Speeding the piece up:

You have to be ready at each level for your challenge. Using the metronome is only going to help if you know what you are doing with your fingering, rests and rhythm, otherwise you could do more harm than good.

Don't try to play the piece at the correct speed yet. Allow yourself to learn how it all fits together, and then gradually build up the speed. (You won't always be playing at such a slow speed, but take your time here and you will be rewarded by finishing learning your music that much quicker.)

If you can do it perfectly at speed number 1, then try it at 1 1/2, but a word of warning…if it starts to break down again, then take it back to the speed you could play it at perfectly and stay with that speed for a little longer before trying again. When this speed has no terrors for you and you can play without mistakes, then put the speed up by one notch or number.

Keep repeating this process. In this way, over time, you will make your target speed. It may take time, but if you go carefully, you will build it back up to the right tempo.

Ready for a game?

One Step Forward and One Step Back:

You will need:

- You and a metronome.

The object of the game:

To speed up your piece.

To play:

The rules for this game are quite straightforward:

- If you can play through your piece at your chosen speed without any breakdowns or uneven playing, then you can move onto the next speed up.

- If you have a minor wobble, then you have to stay at that speed for two more turns.

- If you have a breakdown, then you will have to move the speed down one notch. You start the next practice at your new speed. If you can play through your piece at this speed without any breakdowns you can move the speed up one notch. Any breakdown will result in going *down* a speed again.

This game can be disheartening, as you could have several sessions with the tempo going down rather than up but remember, if you are taking this seriously, the trend will actually be upwards as the week goes on.

Exceeding the speed limit!

If you need to have your piece up to the tempo marked on the page, then you are going to have to try to exceed that speed. The Olympic athletes running 400m have probably practised running 600m too. If they can do the longer distance, then they should be able to manage the shorter one better.

So, you need to try to play faster than the piece suggests, and then, when it comes to performance time, you know that you can easily do the piece at the right speed.

Here are some problems that might arise from going *too fast:*

- Repeating errors - all you will do is reinforce mistakes.
- Missed notes - going too fast for your own good.
- Uneven rhythms - same problem as before.
- Wild intonation - and again.

It is so important to keep your speed sensible that I will repeat my message again:

> Only play at a speed that will let you play it all perfectly.

If you can't play it perfectly, then you really need to go back over the chapter on learning the new piece and repeat the games before attempting to speed it up again.

It may be that, despite all your best efforts, you cannot get the piece up to the target speed. Of course, there are other musical elements to be considered and if these are taken into account, the overall effect may make the piece satisfactory despite not acquiring the speed.

Indeed, it might be better for some students to take a piece at a slightly slower pace rather than sacrifice all the dynamics, rhythms, fingerings, etc., in a bid to win the gold medal for the fastest performance ever. Go, instead, for the most beautiful rendition of the music ever.

To Summarise:

- Play slowly so that you can play perfectly.
- Play the 'One Step Forward, One Step Back' game.

Chapter 8

Getting Your Piece Right

"My teacher says to keep practising my piece until it's right. When will I know it is correct?"

What you need, when trying to finish off a piece, are all the notes, fingering, sharps and flats, slurs, pedalling etc., all correct, but if you try to do all of this in one go, you will just end up in a muddle, and your piece will seem jumbled and unfinished. What you need to do is to tackle one aspect of your music and sort out one issue at a time.

Here is a suggestion to help you focus on one job at a time:

You need to do the **Rollette** game which is on the next page.

The Rollette Game:

For this game you will need:

- A list of the jobs to be done in your music.

- One or two dice depending on the number of jobs on your list.

The object of the game:

To play your music with total focus on the task that was thrown on the die.

To play:

- Make a list of jobs to be done such as the list below.

- Number each of the items on the list.

- Throw your die and see what number comes up.

- Find the item on your list that has the same number as the die.

- You are going to play your music totally focussed on that job, and that job alone.

A list of jobs may look like this:

Correct notes

Correct fingering

Correct rhythm

Quavers and other fast notes played evenly and at the correct tempo

Dynamics

Tone

Phrasing/breathing

Articulation

Tone colour

There are lots more that you can use, but this will give you some idea of the tasks you can focus on.

In the piece of music to be practised this week there are more than six jobs to be done in the music.

1. Correct notes
2. Correct fingering
3. Correct rhythm
4. Quavers and other fast notes to be played evenly at the correct tempo.
5. Dynamics
6. Articulation

For this list you will need one die.

For the other items on your list you will need another die and another list with numbers next to them. You can repeat some of the important items from list 1 as well, such as fingering or rhythm.

Your other list might look like this:

1. Tone colour
2. Phrasing
3. Breathing
4. Steady tempo
5. Notes
6. Quavers passage

The idea is that now you have selected a number and the task that goes with it, then this is what you will be focussing on, and will become the most important thing in the world.

If the die has settled on **2 Correct Fingering** then you will be completely focussed on fingering. This will help you look at the piece of music to make sure the fingering is correct and work on the places where you have been fudging it, and getting in a muddle.

You will play short sections over and over, maybe even a dozen times, insisting on perfect fingering every time.

Remember to work on the fingering without playing any notes so that you can concentrate on your fingers. Pianists might find that they need to change the fingering to make it work fluently. Be prepared to experiment until you find the solution you like.

After half an hour of this, your fingering will be in so much better shape than when you began.

Next lesson, your teacher will most probably comment on how brilliant your fingering is now.

Next time you practise, roll your die again and see what number you get this time. If it has come up with the same number as last time, you can choose to roll the die again so that you work through your piece focussing on a different aspect.

Sometimes, it is worth doing just the bits with, say, slurs or practising just the crescendos and not the rest of the piece at all. For instance, if you are learning slurs, then you could really focus and concentrate on just the slurred notes in your piece to ensure that they are really smooth and not ever so slightly stopping when it gets difficult.

Roll a 2 – Fingering:

A good number to have thrown, even when you think you know your piece quite well. Use this to check:

The key:

Particularly if it is a key you don't like very much, or aren't used to. Check particularly if you have just made a change of key, say from your first exam piece to the second.

Sections with a mass of accidentals:

A collection of flutes could be a 'tootle' but I wonder what the collective noun would be for a lot of sharps or flats in one passage…a 'muddle' of accidentals? Spend a little time with these notes and double check that what you are playing is what is required. Do it slowly and mark in any sharps, flats or naturals while you are checking it out. You could make your music look very attractive by colouring all the F#s in pink, and C#s in blue and so on. It makes it clear to see and easier to identify.

Chords:

Sometimes there are so many notes in a chord that it is impossible to see if you are playing the right thing. Perhaps you are even leaving out something. Check the notes one at a time, building them up from the bottom as though it was the first time you had ever played it.

Broken chord patterns:

It is too easy to focus on the melody and not really notice what is actually going on in the other hand. It may even sound all right, but you might replace a note in an Alberti bass with a wrong note or a different inversion without really noticing. Flute players often get these types of passages and it's all too easy to get a note wrong in the flurry of fingering.

Scale passages:

When you have so many notes in a row, it can be difficult to notice that maybe there is a little skip in the pattern, or that it doesn't finish off the scale, and then you go flying through it wrongly every time. Slow down and be prepared to check, especially if the pattern is broken (composers like doing that to musicians). Keep your eyes open, keep alert for when the scale changes, and be suspicious that you may have missed something. Be ready for surprises, particularly if the music seems to be based around patterns.

Roll a 3 – Rhythm:

It is so easy to almost get the rhythm right. However, if you went into a burger bar and ordered a beef burger, and it was served to you with the filling falling out, and the burger lumpy, you would probably be cross. Or if you bought some pencils and they changed colours unpredictably as you used them, again you'd be complaining. So the same applies to music. If the composer has asked for eight quavers in a row, then he wants them played evenly and steadily. If the composer has asked for dotted crotchets and quaver rhythms then that is what he wants. It is your job to play these notes with the best possible timing.

So the test here is simple…if you wrote out your music as you are playing it, would it look the same as the music on the page? It should. Dotted rhythms can be a problem. It is so common to find sloppy dots. A dotted crotchet gets roughly interpreted as being a bit long and the quaver with it a bit short. Are you guessing what is there or are you really counting 1 and 2 and?

Roll a 5 – Dynamics:

Imagine that you are at school and your voice is stuck at a fairly loud volume. Everything you say will be at that level. So, all day you talk in the same volume all the way through. You greet your friends in the playground with a moderately loud "Hi!" That voice level is all right. Then the teacher takes the register and you answer in the same sound level voice, "Here, Miss." Your voice level is still probably all right. Then your friend whispers a bit of secret gossip, and you reply to her in the same voice level again, "She never did!" Well, that probably wasn't OK. In the next lesson, which happens to be Maths, you are trying to have a secret conversation with your neighbour, but of course, you say in exactly the same voice level, "I hate Maths. It's so boring." Well by now you are probably on your way to a detention or something! Keep on going all day in that same loud voice and you will certainly end up in trouble.

So you see, you have to use different levels of voice throughout your day, and you have to do the same in music. Music is a language that speaks to people without words. Indeed, someone said that music is like a poem. You can say it in one way the first time but the next time you say the poem it will be different. No two readings will be identical. So the same rules of voice level apply. In music they are called dynamics. They make your music exciting and enjoyable. People don't have to listen to your music, but with no variation in the volume level, you can be sure that they won't listen!

Make sure you know what the composer wants.

Composers have usually thought about the volume levels they want to make their music interesting, and will write in their ideas on the score. Check carefully that you are obeying their plans. However, composers often only indicate about five percent of the dynamics they actually want, so don't be afraid to be creative.

Sometimes there is a long stretch of music where nothing seems to happen. Here is a place for you to experiment. If you were back at school and you just spoke all day in a monotone (you know how some people read out loud, with no change in the pitch and as if they are really bored reading the words), well that would be very boring for your friends to listen to as well.

Try out different ideas. You could try a *crescendo* or a *diminuendo*, or varying the dynamics between *forte* and *piano*. Be inventive. Some of the ideas will be horrible, but you may find one or two that really seem to make that section interesting for you, and that is good.

Roll a 4 – Steady Tempo:

This is from the other list with the other die.

If you played your music as if you were a robot it would be very, very steady, but very, very boring. However, if your speed changes uncontrollably from one section to the next, then your audience will feel travel sick as they go up and down the roller coaster of timing.

Watch out for:

- Rushing through the easy notes and then slowing up at the difficult bits.
- Playing well up to the tricky bit and then charging through the horrid bit as fast as possible, hoping it will go away quicker.
- Creeping gradually faster and faster.

The trouble is that if you don't do anything about it, the problem won't go away. How you practise will be the way it will come out when you play it to other people. It will always seem messy, and if you aren't careful, you will just get into a habit of playing it like that, and get so used to hearing it that way that you won't notice it needs attention. Then you'll wonder why your teacher is still going on about the speed of your music.

The secret of success here is to work at the piece SLOWLY. You have to play the piece at such a slow speed that you don't need to change speed at the difficult section. Try playing with a metronome and finding a tempo that allows you to play steadily. When you can play it well at this speed, put the metronome up one notch and try the section at this new speed. Again, when you can play well at this speed, try one more small change of tempo. Over a few days you will gradually get the whole section up to the correct tempo.

Sometimes you have a run of quite easy notes, and you pick up speed, little by little. I remember playing with my flute group. They were playing the tune and a harmony part and I had a lot of quite easy quavers. We could not get this piece right. Eventually I asked the Head of Music to come and conduct for the group and see if he could spot what was happening. After a few minutes of the rehearsal, he stopped the group and said, "Whoever it is that has the quavers…you are gradually creeping faster and faster!" Well, you can guess that I was embarrassed because that was me!

To solve that problem, try using a metronome and establish the tempo. Play through the piece keeping in time with the bleep. Once you get to the end of the section, turn the metronome off, and play it through again, trying to keep to the time in your head. When you get to the end, turn the metronome on again. How does the speed compare this time? Did it feel like the metronome was slowing down? Well that means that you *have* fallen victim to the creep! If the metronome seems as if it has slowed down a lot, then you have speeded up a lot!

Roll a 1 – Tone Colour:

Again, this is on the other die.

Make your music interesting with some changes in tone colour. Imagine different instruments playing different parts. You can imagine the loud sections being played on the cellos, and maybe the dancing quavers played on the violins. It creates a wonderful palette of different colours and feels fun to play too.

"The Rollette game has helped me, but I can't quite tell *how much* it has helped."

Well, try recording your piece. Roll one of your dice to find out what you are going to focus on when you listen to the recording. If you chose Correct Notes, then this is what you will be listening out for when you hear your piece. How does it sound? Are the notes good and crystal clear, or do they sound muddled? Are they rushed, or keeping a good, steady tempo? Your task here is to make a quick judgement about what you liked and what worked and didn't work.

Try recording it again with that same focus in mind. See if you are happier with this second attempt than before. Remember that you are only listening to the correct notes at this stage; don't let other numbers start shouting out about other problems.

"What do I do next?"

The next step is to try to listen to two targets at the same time. This is tricky, but you can do it if you have worked through thoroughly using one at a time. By the time you come to perform this piece you will need to have worked through all your numbers, so it makes sense to start to build up your piece with correct notes and dynamics, or the correct tempo and tone colour. Don't try too many numbers at once, but gradually build up your piece by rolling the two dice several times and noting the numbers they come up with. You will then target those numbers from your list. Eventually, you will have rolled all the numbers and you will have completed looking in detail at your music.

To Summarise:

> Work **thoroughly** and **thoughtfully** through all the items on the list of jobs to be done for your piece by playing **ROLLETTE.**

Chapter 9

Quality Not Quantity

Well done, you have got your piece up to an amazing standard. You have learned all the floors in the skyscraper, and played all the numbers in Rollette. Already you have done work that you should be truly pleased with.

Now, how will it stand up to being played at a lesson? How ready is it for a performance?

How many times I have heard my pupils say, "It went so much better at home!" Somehow, there is a difference between how you manage at home and, with the slight increase in pressure, playing in a lesson, even to your teacher who you know really well.

If you really want to know what happens to your brain, then it is all in my book *Mind Over Matter* (Whykes, 2007), but here is a short excerpt from it:

> You will be surprised to learn that maybe this all started when you were a child, when you were complimented for doing something well that you enjoyed doing.
>
> The next time you engaged in that activity you probably didn't feel so comfortable about doing it, and felt slightly less confident about it.

What happened? It was because the focus of your satisfaction in the activity shifted from internal, where you were experiencing the inner sense of enjoyment of being 'in flow' and at one with the activity, to an external one, as you experienced the response from outside. Once these signals became entangled, the more subtle inner satisfaction feelings can get pushed into the background. What we are left with is the sense of being judged, from whence performance anxiety is but a short step away.

Wow! Well, it all boils down to this: you were playing along, and just enjoying yourself. The music was OK, the fingering reasonable, the counting wasn't really happening, and you were just enjoying the process. That's fine. But then, along came your first challenge like counting it right, and now you know how it should be counted. You and your teacher will be cross if the counting goes all wrong next time, so now you have just a little bit of pressure. Now the music isn't going along quite as happily as before.

The more levels of difficulty you add to your music, having built both a **skyscraper** and done the **Rollette** game, the more pressure you feel to keep the music correct. This is all very well until there is a *little more* pressure in showing how you have worked on the music when you come to play it in the lesson.

"It's all right when I play it at home!"

How are we going to overcome this? How are we going to get this piece of music from where it is now, to making it consistent enough to play for a concert or an exam, or even just for your teacher?

You need to see HOW you perform under pressure and WHERE the piece does and doesn't work. (One good thing about this chapter is that after you have completed it you will never feel so anxious again about playing it to anyone; indeed, it may seem positively easy!)

"It's all right when I play it at home," goes the cry. That's because there is no pressure at home when you are practising. Go to your lesson, and there is pressure to achieve, to show your teacher how well you have worked, and then your music doesn't work. To be honest, it probably did sound like this at home, but because you were your own judge, you may have thought that it was good enough.

So, we need to put pressure on AT HOME so that mistakes that happen at practice time get noticed, practised and eliminated.

Boiling Eggs.

My piano teacher used to say to me that I would be hopeless at boiling an egg. I would get the saucepan ready, have the water boiling away, collect the egg from the box, get the spoon ready to eat the egg with, but actually never cook the egg. Well, to be honest, I didn't know what he meant, but one day it dawned on me.

He was saying that I spent a great deal of time playing through the piece, getting dynamics, *staccati*, slurs and expression into the piece, (getting the pan, water and egg ready) but because I didn't practise just the hard bits, they never got better (so I never put the egg into the pan to cook it!).

I learnt how to take the time to target these bits, being prepared to go over the notes many times (actually cooking the egg!). I learnt how to play the section through until I got it right (playing) and then had to play it 10 times perfectly before I could stop (practice). If I went wrong, then I had to return to the beginning and start playing and counting to 10 all over again.

This certainly put my playing under some pressure, especially as I reached the ninth time.

Now it's time to introduce some pressure into *your* practice time!

Games Time

Most of these games have a common theme, which is that *your practice session is over once the game is won.*

If you want to finish your practice and have some free time then you have to play the game well but the game can only go reasonably well if you have practised properly in the first place. You will find these games go better if:

- You take care over your speed and play slowly and carefully.
- You do small and manageable chunks, for every extra bit you add will increase the amount that could go wrong.
- You take care with your fingering. You probably will find that, if your fingering is a bit hit-or-miss, you will be playing the game for hours. Stick to the fingering that works.
- You think and visualise what you are going to do before you begin playing.
- You find out what causes the tricky bit to fail in the first place.

Some of these games are harder than others, but you *can* do them. Think positive. If you think that the play-through will go well, then it probably will go well.

Game 1: Downfall

This is a good (but mean) game to discover whether you know a particular passage or not. Only do this one if you are feeling brave.

You will need:

- A strip of paper divided into eight squares vertically. The top square will be 1 and the bottom one will be Home.

- A token.

The object of the game:

To move your token from 1 to Home.

To play:

- Number the squares.

- Place your token on square 1.

- Choose a passage to test.

- Play through this passage. If you played it perfectly then you can move your token down one square.

- Play through the test piece again. If you played it without mistakes then move the token down another square.

- If anything goes wrong then you go back up a square (unless you went wrong on the first go, in which case you stay there.)

- Keep going like this until you get to Home.

Congratulations! You have finished!

Because the object of the game is to play without errors, this can be such a difficult game to complete, but you have to finish it. Don't give up at square 6.

Remember that these games are about putting pressure on your work to see how reliable it is. The problem is that, as you get near the end of the game you really want to finish and go. You get to square 5 and you worry and are keen to get the game finished, and then there is a little error. Back up one square you go!

Now you get annoyed. You were so close to being able to pack up and go, and now you are back at square 4!

The next thing you probably do is go faster so that you can finish. This will lead to another failure and back you go to square 3!

You can see that this game is aptly and ironically named 'Downfall'. Any mistake and it is your downfall. Remember this game is not over until you get to Home, so this rewards pupils that can always get their piece right, but is doom and gloom to anyone who can't.

There is an upside to this, you will be pleased to hear. Once you have played this game several times you will find yourself getting quite nervous as you approach the final stages, but you will discover that it is not nerves that stop you from finishing but how well you know the passage. You will practise being nervous, while knowing that your pieces have survived even the dreaded 'Downfall' game.

In any of the games you can take <u>time out</u> so that you can work out what is going wrong. You can have as along as you like to correct any issues. The game doesn't start again until you call <u>time in</u>, at which point you can carry on with the game.

The next game tests how well you know much more substantial chunks of your piece, or indeed, all of it.

Game 2: In the Pot

You will need:

- Two small pots (jam jar, cups or even a couple of saucers will do).
- 10 tokens.

The object of the game:

To move all the tokens into pot 2.

To play:

- You choose a big chunk, or all, of the music.
- Put all the tokens into pot 1.
- Play your piece through.
- If you were successful, with NO mistakes, wobbly bits or wrong fingerings, then you can put one token into pot 2.
- Every time you are successful, transfer another token to pot 2.
- Every time you make a mistake, you have to take a token from pot 2 and place it in pot 1.
- The game is finished when all the tokens have been transferred to pot 2.
- Time out can be called to stop and analyse any problems that occur.
- Time in has to be called to re-enter the game.

This is a really frustrating game especially if you go wrong on time number 9, but really builds up fluency in the piece.

Game 3: Teddy Bear

You will need:

- A die.
- A teddy bear.
- A pencil and paper for keeping score.

The object of the game:

The first one to 30 points wins.

To play:

- You throw the die first, e.g. 4.
- Play your piece through and if it goes correctly, you get all 4 points.
- (Only 26 more points to go!)
- You get another go, so throw again, e.g. 6.

- If you got it right you get the points on the die.
- If you go wrong then Teddy gets the 6 points.
- This makes the score 4 to you and 6 to Teddy.
- You throw again and keep playing the game like this until either you or Teddy gets to 30 points.

A variation of this game is to play it with two dice instead, or another person instead of a Teddy. Choose the target score yourself this time.

For the next game you can choose how **much** or **little** you do. It could be one level of a skyscraper or a whole piece.

Game 4: Noughts and Crosses

You will need:

- Paper.

- Pencil.

- A parent or other adult.

The object of the game:

To win the game of noughts and crosses.

To play:

- Draw a noughts and crosses grid like this **#**.

- You choose the target section of music and play carefully.

- If there were no mistakes you get to put an **X** on the grid.

- If you messed up then your parent gets to put their **O** on the grid.

- If you got it right, you get another turn.

- Repeat the same section. If you get it right again, then you put your next **X** on the grid.

- Keep going until you've finished the grid.

- Aim to win the best of **three** games.

If you lose or draw don't worry, but find out what let your work down. You have five minutes <u>time out</u> to correct your problem and then you can have a rematch.

Game 5: Marathon

This is a slightly different game from the others, in that there is no actual penalty for errors.

You will need:

- Yourself, your instrument and your music.

The object of the game:

To complete one circuit of your piece from any random bar without mistakes.

To play:

- Choose any bar of your piece at random.

- You start playing from here.

- Continue to the end of the piece then return to the beginning of the piece and play until you arrive back at your start bar.

Were there any mistakes?

- Take note of how many errors there were, e.g. 7

Another complete circuit:

- Take a <u>Time Out</u> and correct any errors.

- You now do another lap of your piece, but you can only have 6 mistakes now. Every time you do Marathon, you have to make fewer mistakes than the time before until you can do a perfect circuit.

- Continue until you manage one perfect lap.

80

Game 6: Consequences

This should take place as the **last** of the practice session activities.

You will need:

- You and your music.
- A parent or another adult.

The object of the game:

To play your piece, or the section you have been practising, perfectly, even if it is slowly.

To play:

- Concentrate hard.
- Play your work all through to an adult.
- If you play perfectly, you can stop.
- If you mess up, you have to do five more minutes, but then you are allowed to stop.

To make any of the games harder you can:

- Make the sections longer.
- Play with a metronome.
- Play with very clear delivery.
- Play from memory.
- Change the time limit that you have used.

To Summarise:

To see how your pieces will stand up under pressure try playing the games:

Downfall
In the Pot
Teddy Bear
Noughts and Crosses
Marathon
Consequences

Chapter 10

Scales

"I really like playing my pieces, but my teacher makes me work on boring scales and exercises as well. Why do I have to do them? Why can't I just concentrate on proper pieces of music instead?"

You need to practise scales and exercises if you want to develop a good technique. Without proper fingering technique you will never be able to play music really well. So if you want to become a better player, you need to get working on them.

Scales are not:

- Just bits of torture that teachers like to give out so that practice can get even more boring!
- Just finger exercises.

Scales are:

- Amazingly good for your brain, because the more scales you know, the more key signatures you will also know. This means that you will know and feel reasonably comfortable with the way your fingers have to work on the keys and the stretches or twists and turns you need to make the scale work.

Scales and arpeggios are part of most exam syllabuses. They are perhaps the most difficult aspect of musical development because we look at them with anything from mild distaste to absolute loathing.

Regrettably scales are a fundamental part of technique because they teach that area of musicianship that includes the control of all physical movement involved in playing an instrument or singing. Technique also controls tone, tone colour, intonation, dynamic level and rhythm. It is not merely a set of isolated physical or mechanical tasks because these link in to your actual performance. No matter how well intentioned a player may be, and no matter how well they have practised, the performance of the piece will fall down if it isn't technically secure. Those subtle shadings of dynamics or rhythms will not stand up to being performed if the technique is not there.

Here are some reasons pupils have given *for* learning scales:

- "Scales improve technique, making my fingers work better, and helping me control my tone and articulation."
- "They speed up the learning of new pieces because so many pieces have scales and arpeggios in them."
- "I can sight-read better now because I can see the pattern when there is a scale or arpeggio in the music."
- "I get good marks in exams because I can play my scales well."
- "Scales help me understand and build a sense of key."

The problem with scales is that they can be boring and it is possible to spend a lot of time on them and for them not to improve.

How to learn scales:

By ear or not by ear?

In exams, scales have to be played off by heart, and so students are encouraged to play them without the music. However, it is useful to know what they look like too, since this is the form we find them in written music, and essential for a good sight-reading technique.

Scales should not be learnt by feeling your way through the notes, because this will result in mistakes and unrhythmic playing. If you have to play them two or three times then you just don't know them.

A memorised scale has to be built up by many careful and thoughtful play-throughs. What you are after is being able to play them through without thinking about them any more than you need to think about tying your shoelaces. You learnt to do this by a series of small steps. So it is with learning scales.

Learning scales without learning scales:

- Write down the note names of the scale. Your mind needs to make a connection between the note name, the note written on the page and the physical action that is required to produce it.
- Say the names of the notes out loud, including any accidentals, both ascending and descending.
- Say the names of the notes and finger the scale, without bowing or blowing, or on the lid of a piano.
- Play the scale slowly and carefully.

One problem is that you don't always know what the scale should *sound* like, so then you might not even know whether you are playing it correctly or not.

- You will need your teacher to play the first five notes of the scale to you, slowly in your lesson.
- It might be good to record these notes, otherwise you will have to listen carefully so that you can remember them.
- You have to sing these notes in your head, slowly.
- Now sing them out loud and work at them until you have the notes and intervals correct.
- Now play these notes by ear.
- When this stage is correct you can try the first octave.

Use this system to learn your arpeggios and other scale patterns too, listening carefully to the shape and pattern.

The Ladder Method:

Another method for learning scales is to play part of the scale, e.g. the first five notes ascending and descending slowly and carefully.

Then run a self-check to see if you can do that section well.

Use a metronome to test out whether you can play this part of the scale. You have to play one note per beat, so choose a sensible speed and think carefully before you begin. If you can't play it without mistakes of any kind then you have to put the speed down a notch and do the scale again twice at that slower speed. If you are successful at your first attempt then the speed can go up a notch.

Once you are confident with these first five notes, then you add the next note up, thus giving you six notes of your scale. Check it again with the metronome, but remember to reset the speed to something a little slower to allow you to play it perfectly.

Having successfully added the sixth note, you go on and add the seventh note and so on until you have covered the notes required for that scale. (This is a good method for pianists learning those difficult contrary motion scales.)

If you have tricky fingerings or new notes to add, perhaps at the top of a flute scale, then start at the top note and add the next note down. Play them several times slowly and thoughtfully, going up and down until you feel you have mastered these two notes and their fingerings. Then add the next note down to give you three top notes. Play them several times, again taking great care with fingering. You keep adding a note to the ones you have already worked on, until you have achieved the top octave. Take your time and it will pay dividends.

Practise going over the top of the scale too. For example: start with the leading note of the scale, then play the next note up (which is the upper tonic note) and return to the leading note. Next time play the sub-mediant, the leading, then the tonic and work back to the sub-mediant. As you work at the scale keep adding notes either side of the upper tonic. This pattern is like an arc and builds up your confidence with the upper notes of a scale.

When you are working on scales be aware of the danger of pausing before a difficult note. Woodwind players can find themselves taking a tiny breath before the awkward tone and a half interval in minor scales. Use the metronome to help overcome this habit.

Know Your Scales:

Strangely, knowing your scales will help you find the correct notes in a sight-reading piece more easily. If you know your scales, you should be able to say what sharps or flats you will need and what other notes are likely to be required too. If you are playing in A major then you would expect to find an F#, a C# and a G#, and not too many B flats!

Music is made up of patterns, and if you can see the key (or scale) that you are working in, then you can make some guesses about what notes are likely to be found and what aren't.

If you practise the scale in the same key as the piece of music you are going to play then you will familiarise yourself with the requirements of sharps or flats that you will need. The more you practise the scale, the more comfortable you will feel with the music too.

Here is a tip for singers and instrumental players: try hearing the next note in your head before playing it. This will help you keep in tune.

Scales are made up of tones and semitones (whole and half steps), but you need a little more information than just **knowing** that semitones are adjacent notes; you need to be able to **hear** and **sing** them too.

Quirky Things:

You need to get to know the quirky things about each scale. Whatever your instrument, there are usually things that you can remember about them. Make a list of the funny things about the scale you are learning... for instance:

F major on the piano, hands together:

- Right hand 4th finger is going on the B flat.
- Right hand ends on 4th finger.
- Thumbs go together on the F in the middle.

F# minor on the flute:

- Has three sharps.
- Starts on F#, so use the ring finger.
- E is sharp, so gets fingered like an F natural.
- There feels like a big jump from D to E sharp because it feels like D to F natural.

So, before you play the scale, think about the quirky things that make this scale so different from any other scale that you know.

Put a silly picture with the scale:

This is a well-known memory trick that helps you associate the thing you need to remember with an image. You could have a picture of a cactus in your mind when you think of F# minor. B flat major could look like a bicycle with two wobbly wheels, one for each flat!

Dos and Don'ts:

- If you want to get rid of your scales practice quicker, then always make sure that you double-check that you have the correct notes and fingering.
- Pianists, listen out for your thumb notes (where you place your thumb as you go up and down the scale)...you shouldn't hear them! Check your technique is letting you move your fingers out of the way as you place your thumb.
- Instrumentalists should listen for co-ordinating the tongue and fingers together...try the scale notes *staccato* and slowly. This will prevent them from going dth dth.
- Ask yourself if all the fingers work at the strength and speed as all the others. 4th and 5th fingers tend to be the weakest.
- Play your scales as *legato* as possible. Make any join between registers really smooth with both breath and speed of fingers. Pianists should listen out for where your fingers overlap by leaving one finger down as you start to play the next.

"What is the perfect scale?"

- A scale should always be played with an even tone.
- It should be played with dynamics that make the scale feel as if it is played with a gentle arc that gives a sense of direction but without over enthusiastic *crescendo* and *diminuendo*.
- You should be careful that the quality of the sound stays good and controlled, especially at the change of direction.
- The first and last notes should not have any accents.
- You need to play with a secure rhythm and stable pulse, again taking care as you change direction.
- In *staccato* scales, notes should always be played lightly and all of the same length with no accents.
- If you play an instrument where you have to worry about tuning, scales must always be played in tune.
- All the scales should be played at the same tempo.

"How should I practise my scales?"

You need to listen carefully to what you are playing to make sure you notice any inconsistencies of tone, rhythm or dynamics or you won't be able to get them perfect as quickly as you'd like.

Here are some tried and tested strategies for learning your scales:

- Practise using different rhythms, dynamics and articulation. There are plenty of variations so you don't need to keep doing it the same way at all.
- Vary the tempo: slow tempo for improving tone and intonation and fast for developing fingering and fluency.
- Vary the articulation by playing in groups of two, three, four, six or eight, to develop evenness and control.
- Start at the top of the scale and do the descending side before ascending, instead of always starting at the bottom.
- Try beginning your scale on any note. For example, if you are learning F major, then start on B flat and play from there up to the next B flat...don't go off into B flat major though, stay in F major. (This is a tricky idea, but it will make you think in

terms of the key you are in, and only works if you know your scale rather than feeling and hoping your way.)

- Play them *staccato* ascending and *legato* descending, and the other way round.
- Pianists can torture themselves by playing one hand *legato* while playing *staccato* in the other and with a different dynamic level in each hand too.

Another problem with scales is that we spend a good deal of time playing the ones we are already good at and leave out the ones we are not so keen on, so G major gets better and better while G minor gets left undone. No wonder that, when we get to the lesson, we don't seem to have done as much work as our teacher had hoped.

Here is a game for you to test out how well you know your scales:

The Three Pot Game

Before you start:

- You will need a complete list of your scales (plus arpeggios and chromatic scales). Check with the appropriate list below to see how to go about it.
- Choose the style of game that is appropriate for you from the following lists:

List 1 for instrumentalists

Suppose your list of scales and arpeggios consists of C, G, F, A minor and G minor. You will need one for each of the scales played tongued, one for each scale played slurred and one for each arpeggio. You will need 20 slips here.

However, you might find it easier to have a pot with just scales and another with a random mixture of slips saying tongued or slurred (and *staccato* if appropriate).

List 2 for pianists (if you use hands together)

Suppose your list of scales and arpeggios comprises C#, G, F major, A flat minor and G minor. Take C# major scale for example; you will need one slip for C# major played with your right hand, the same scale with the left hand and one for both hands together. That makes three slips. In this example you have 5 scales with three slips each, giving a pot with 15 slips. Remember to do the same thing for your arpeggios. You will need one slip for each hand separately and hands together, making 3 slips for every arpeggio.

List 3 for other pianists (who only need one hand at a time)

Suppose your list of scales comprises C, G, F, A minor and G minor. Take C major scale for example; you will need one slip for C major played with your right hand, and one for C major with the left hand. That makes two slips. In this particular example you have 5 scales and 5 arpeggios with two slips each, giving a pot with 20 slips.

You will need:

- 3 pots.
- Paper, pencil and scissors.
- A timer (on your watch or mobile phone).

The object of the game:

To get all the scales into pot 3.

Before you play:

- Write the name of all the scales on the piece of paper and cut it out so they are on a slip of paper each.
- Put them all into pot 1.
- Instrumentalists will also need slips of paper with 'tongued', 'slurred' and '*staccato*'.

To play

- You are going to play for 10 minutes so put the timer on.

- Pick a scale out of pot 1. (Also pick an articulation style if necessary.) Think about it and then play it.

- If you play it perfectly then the scale slip goes into pot 2.

- If you don't play it perfectly, then work out what you need to do in order to get it correct. Play it 3 times correctly. Then it can go into pot 2.

- If it still didn't work, then the slip goes into pot 3.

- Keep picking slips out of pot 1, playing the scales and transferring them to pot 2 as before.

- When the timer goes off, you STOP.

- If you didn't finish all the scales, at the next practice you carry on picking out scales from pot 1. If you have finished all the scales in pot 1, then transfer all of them back from pot 2 to pot 1 and start all over again. Any bad scales go back into pot 3.

- On the third day, when you practise your scales, remember to work on pot 3 scales only. Remember the note names, the quirky things and the pictures you associate with them.

- At the end of this session all the scales are returned to pot 1 to begin all over again.

- **If you want to make this game more competitive**, you score 10 points for every perfect scale, 5 for every scale that needed another go but went into pot 2, and take 5 off for every scale that ended up in pot 3.
- Your aim will be to get a perfect score.

This game works well, because the scales get the amount of practice they deserve. The ones you know really well you should sail through, and you score good points whereas the ones that are not well enough known will get more work.

You can do any of the other games as well that we had in an earlier chapter…how about **Downfall?**

"I think I know my scales now."

Well, let's test them out:

1. Pianists, can you play two different scales at the same time, like E major in the right hand and F in the left? It will sound terrible but, if you can do it, then congratulations! You can pick two scales at random.
   Other instrumentalists can pick two scales at random, and play one ascending and the other descending. You could play C major ascending and then D major descending.
2. Now play your scales with your eyes shut and imagine what your fingers are doing. This is fine for pianists since you can remember and visualise the black and white keys and it will help you understand the layout of the scale. It is harder for instrumentalists because you will have to work hard to visualise what each finger movement should be.
3. Play them without the instrument. Can you picture how your fingers and hands have to move?
4. Play the scale for as many octaves as you possibly can – pianists can zoom up and down the whole keyboard. Instrumentalists

may only be able to do a couple, but you can keep going up in the same scale as far as you can manage: 17, 18 or 19 notes.

5. Miss out every fifth note, for example F major will go F, G, A, B flat - D, E, F, G - etc. When you can do this, then try leaving out a different numbered note.

There are one or two useful books that you could buy that could help you learn your scales, some of which come with play-along CDs. However, whatever you do, nothing will change the fact that you have to be careful, sensible and hard working in order to get your scales up to a good standard.

To Summarise:

- Learn your scales as you would learn spellings: write them out in both notation and in letter names, saying the note names out loud.
- Finger them without playing them out loud.
- Play the **Three Pot game**.
- Play **Downfall** or any of the games from Chapter 9. (See Index for list of games.)

Chapter 11

Listening

Throughout this book the word listening has occurred many times: listening to yourself playing your scales, in owning your own music and in learning the notes. It is an important skill and one that you need to practise.

Do you remember that list of the ways we learn? We learn by doing, and seeing but we also learn by listening. Just as we learn how to do something, so we need to learn how to do listening. The best way for musicians to learn to listen is to learn to sing back what we hear.

"But I can't sing."

There are really very few people who are truly unable to sing back a note, or who are really tone deaf.

Here is a simple exercise for those who feel they can only sing one note, or groan, but you will need a piano or a keyboard. You sing a note and then quickly find it on the piano. Play the note and listen carefully as the sound begins to die away and sing again, repeating this until it becomes reliable.

Sometimes you will find that you sing a different note when trying to sing back the original note, but this is fine. Just try to focus on the sound as the note dies away and try to find it in your voice by squeezing or relaxing your throat muscles.

Once you have sung your note back reasonably correctly, then you are going to try and sing 'nee-naw, nee-naw' like an ambulance or police car, trying to end on your note. You may find this takes time before you feel confident but keep working on it and it will pay dividends.

To extend your range you need to try simple exercises like singing the first few notes of *'Doh, a deer'*. Then try *'London's Burning'* and then *'Twinkle Twinkle, Little Star'*. Take care with these exercises and your confidence will build.

"How do I learn to play and sing in tune?"

You should do this pitch exercise regularly so that you keep working on your intonation (being neither too sharp nor too flat in pitch).

Concentrate on a single interval such as the first four notes of *'Twinkle, Twinkle (Little Star)'*, which is an interval of five notes (a fifth). First hear the interval in your head, then sing it out loud and then play it. Do the same with *'Away (in a Manger)'*, which is a fourth; try a sixth - *'Twinkle, Twinkle Little Star'*: a seventh - *'Somewhere Over the Rainbow'* and an octave - *'Some-where (Over the Rainbow)'*. Do a second - *'Frère Jacques'* and a third - *'Doh a deer, a female deer,'* too.

When you play your scales you should hear and sing each note *before* you play it.

One of the problems with aural (listening) tests in exams is that they rely heavily on what we call short-term memory. This memory is a temporary storage unit that can remember small chunks of information (words, numbers or letters) for about 20 seconds. This doesn't appear to be of much use to a musician. After all, why should we want to remember our music for only 20 seconds or so?

Well, if there is already some information stored in your long-term memory then your brain makes a very fast connection between the two memories, which helps you understand the information and it will go into your long-term memory. So you need to feed your brain with information prior to doing aural tests.

It works like this: if you have learnt your intervals from the pitch exercise then you have fed your long-term memory with information about what thirds or seconds sound like. In the 'singing back like an echo' aural test, you hear several notes and have to sing them back. You put them into your short-term memory. If you have already learnt what these intervals sound like and they are stored in your long-term memory, then your brain can make a connection. It says, "I've heard this before," makes the link and then you can sing it back confidently.

You can practise singing back small sections of melodies if you start by playing only a couple of notes and then singing them back. Try playing three random notes and singing those back for a few days, and after that spend a few days doing four notes at random. Keep building up the number of notes in your sequence up to about eight notes. This is harder than doing the actual test in an exam because the melodies you get in an exam are more likely to form a pattern that is easier to remember than your random notes.

You should try to listen to music often and with understanding. Even music that goes with advertisements can be a worthwhile opportunity to listen carefully. Try to describe what happens. Maybe it begins with a piano playing the main tune *staccato* and *pianissimo*. Perhaps there is a drumbeat in the background and then a guitar joins in.

What happens in your favourite pop-song? Listen carefully and tell yourself what you hear in the introduction!

To Summarise:

- Try to listen carefully to any type of music.
- Ask yourself what happens in the background, and what dynamics are used?
- Learn to sing the intervals of the scale, both next-door notes and jumping from the tonic to other notes.

Chapter 12

Memorising Music

The famous pianist, Franz Liszt, seems to have been responsible for the requirement for musicians to play from memory. There are some situations where it *is* necessary for the musician to play without music, for instance if you are a soloist at *The Proms*, or for a music festival.

It is probably true to say that most musicians, of any standard, will play more pleasingly when they can just listen to what they are doing rather than being involved in de-coding the notes on the page. So let's work at how to memorise music.

There are various schemes we employ when we learn something off by heart. Some students learn by seeing patterns in a piece of music. For instance, in spelling, some people always remember 'together' is made up of *to-get-her*. They see patterns in pieces of music, scales and chords, and remember them.

Some pupils use their listening skills a lot. Some people can hear a piece of music and remember it well enough to be able to reproduce it later. Mozart was incredibly good at this sort of thing.

There are folk who solve the problem of music by using their understanding of scales, arpeggios, broken chords and the like.

Others actually seem to be able to remember what music looks like on the page, seeing it like a photograph.

"Can I learn music off by heart?"

When we commit things to memory we use a mixture of these ideas: you will need to **see** what you are doing, you will need to **hear** what you are doing and you will need to **know** what happens in the music that you are playing.

1. Watch your fingers.

I'm about to get into trouble here because a lot of piano teachers tell you to keep focussed on the music and not to watch your hands. Well, I am about to give you some reasons why it may be a good idea to see what you are doing!

Pianists: You can watch your hands whenever you need to. It is better to look and check your hands are in the right place than ploughing along not really knowing if you are playing any of the right notes. Unfortunately, you cannot watch both your hands and the music, so at the very least you need to know the notes off by heart so you can watch your hands.

Instrumentalists: You can turn your instrument around so that you can see what you are doing. Flute players can put their instrument on their left shoulder. All players need to be able to watch their fingers from time to time.

2. Listen to what you are playing.

Many times, we play through our music and couldn't even begin to say anything about it when we have finished! So, it would be good to learn a bit off by heart so you can really appreciate what you are producing. You see famous players apparently staring off into the distance as they play, but what they are doing is listening intently to their performance. After all, they have worked hard to make every note beautiful and clear when they have been practising and they want to listen carefully to check that their music is going as well as possible. (They are also in 'the zone'. See *Let's Perform* for more about being in the zone.) It is easier to do this if you are not trying to read the notes at the same time.

3. Know what you are doing.

You can't play from memory unless you have worked hard on the music, and really this is what you have done by going slowly and repeatedly over your targeted practice. You will play with so much more confidence and freedom if you play from memory. Even if you actually use the music when you perform your pieces, the fact that you know your music so well will give you an added edge.

4. Look more confident.

If you had to choose between one pupil who can play their music perfectly with their copy in front of them and the other pupil who plays the same music perfectly from memory, you probably would award the player doing it off by heart the premier place. It just looks so much better.

"How can I learn to play from memory?"

Actually, as you have worked steadily through the ideas in the earlier chapters in this book, you have probably got to know your piece really well. However, here are some tools to help you:

1. Visualisation:

This is a very powerful tool that helps with problem solving. In your mind, play through the section you are working on. Did you manage it or did you need a peep at the music to help you on your way? If you had to look, then you don't really know it off by heart, and that very bit where your memory failed you is probably the very bit you still need to work on.

Go back and try **Downfall** or **Noughts and Crosses** to encourage yourself to really get to grips with this section.

2. The Moving Book:

Choose only a small section to learn first. Now make your music harder to read. You can read it as much as you like but you are going to gradually move your book further away.

Start off with the book on the music stand as usual, but after a few days move it onto a chair or the piano stool next to you. You can still read it, but now you can't read it so easily.

After a few more days, place the music on the floor in front of you, then a few days later move it behind you; later put it at the other side of the room, etc. I am sure you have got the idea by now.

3. Describing the music:

To be able to play it well, you need to be able to describe what the music is doing. Choose a couple of bars and try to explain exactly what is happening. Can you say exactly what the notes are? Can you describe the rhythm, and say what the pattern of the notes is?

Can you, starting at the key and time signatures, write out the music? You will be surprised at how much you rely on your fingers to play the piece and how little 'thinking' you do when playing from memory. What happens is that your brain remembers which muscles have to be used and when, and so you remember the music when you finger it. Take the fingering away and all of a sudden it is a lot harder to remember. However, it is a really useful exercise to have to write in the rests, the sharps or flats and dynamics. You will have to visualise the music, call it into your mind's 'eye'. You may well have to airplay your instrument in order to recall the notes.

When you are playing from memory, the very bits that let you down may respond well to being written out and thus clarify your understanding of those sections.

Try to keep the passages that you are memorising to short, containable sections, so that, when you play, you are playing short bits joined together rather than thinking of it as being one whole, long piece.

4. Jigsaw Puzzles:

Don't be afraid to work at your piece in bits, like a jigsaw puzzle. We often begin at the beginning and work through to the end. The problem with this method is that the beginning gets better and better, because it gets played so often and the ending is weak because we hardly ever get there due to stopping at an error and starting again. Remember to play the **Jigsaw Puzzle** game from chapter 4 and the **Marathon** game to prevent this from happening.

5. A Quick Sketch:

This may seem a bit random at first glance, but what you do is learn what happens in the piece as a rough sketch. You get to know the opening, you know roughly how the middle section goes and you can describe the ending. Now you can start to add some details, for example, learning that the first set of arpeggios start on G, but the second start on D, and the higher group starting on G are the quieter ones, and the D set *crescendo* towards the end. Now you could reconstruct the whole passage if you wanted to, not having to rely on momentum or fingering but on an understanding of how the whole piece is put together.

Here is a **technique** for helping to memorise your music. This will work particularly well if you do one bar at a time:

1. Look for a few moments at the bar you want to remember.
2. Look away from the music.
3. Then, moving your eyes up and to the left, imagine and remember the notes in the music.
4. Look back at the original music to fill in any missing notes and correct any part of the music that you didn't see in your mind.
5. Repeat the process until you can easily visualise the correct bar in your mind.
6. It may help to position the music up and to your left, a little way away from you.
7. You can imagine the notes in bright colours if you like.
8. Look away again, look up at your mental image and then write out your music.
9. If it is not correct, then go back to step 1 and repeat the process from the beginning.

This sounds quite complicated at first, but you will be surprised at how well you will be able to recall the bar.

To Summarise:

- Visualise your music; remember how it feels and how it looks.
- Write it out.
- Say what happens in it.
- Try the learning technique to help recall the music.

Chapter 13

Organising Your Time

> Time is more valuable than money. You can get more money but
> you can't get more time.
>
> Jim Rohn

In this chapter we will look at how to manage:

- Your weekly practice.
- How to plan for the big day.

At the end of your lesson you should be going home with a notebook
that has clear notes concerning your tasks for the week and a mind full of
information and ideas. However, what you really could do with are:

- The actual tasks you need to do.
- The practice tools you will need.
- How to tell when you have finished your tasks.

BUT you will also need to know *how* to go about practising. After all,
you have had a lesson for one day in the week with your teacher telling
you what to do and then you have six more days all on your own, and
a list of jobs to be done. What order do you do the jobs in? What
happens to the list if you get stuck with a tricky bit? How should you
use an unexpected practice opportunity? How should you allocate your
time to make sure that all your jobs on your list get done? You might

try hard, but without knowing how and what to practise, you might get to the end of the week and still not get all the tasks finished.

You were neither born with an automatic understanding of how to break up tasks into manageable chunks, nor with information about how to timetable your work for an exam or concert.

You need a proper planner. There are several at the end of this book for you to photocopy for your **weekly** work, **weekly planner plus rewards day** and one for the preparation for a **Big Day.**

Now it would be good if your teacher looked at your weekly planner, and filled it in with you since, in this way, you will feel as if you are more in charge of what you have to do and when you are going to do it. If, however, they prefer to give you a list of tasks, then you will have to split them up for yourself. This is what you did as your first task before building your skyscraper.

However, what you need to know is, "how am I doing? Am I on track? Am I going to be ready for my lesson?"

You are going to plan out your work in your planner (see photocopiable blank planners at the end of this book).

The Weekly Planner:

You have to break up the tasks set by your teacher into chunks as discussed in the chapter on Begin to Build a Skyscraper. Split up your work and fill in your planner. Now you can see what work needs to be done on days 1 and 2.

If you have completed your first set of tasks by day 2 then you are on track. If you have not completed it, then you need to adjust the time you are spending practising and maybe how you are doing it to get back on track since you will still need to complete the list of jobs before your next lesson.

Apply some pressure games to make sure the music will stand up to being played to someone else. (See the chapter called Quality Not Quantity for some games to try to make your piece reliable.)

Here is an example, using your teacher's list from the chapter on Learning the Notes:

The Weekly Planner

Date	Piece 1	Piece 2	Piece 3	Scales	Aural	Theory
			Lesson Time			
	First page of Mozart Flute Sonata **Tools:** Skyscraper: all floor levels	Tidy up Study 17 – slurs, *staccati* and dynamics **Tools:** Rollette	Rondeau Quavers must be accurate and even **Tools:** Distorted rhythms	Learn F major scale and arpeggio	Sing 5 notes of scale	Exercises 17 - 20
Day 1	Bars 1 - 4	Make a list of jobs and play Rollette	Play long/ short pattern	Write and learn notes of scale	Sing up and down 5 notes	Ex. 17
Day 2	Bars 5 - 8 Revise bars 1 - 4	Rollette: Slurs	Play short/long pattern	Name notes and finger scale	Sing scale; jump from note 1 to 3	Ex. 18
Day 3	Bars 9 - 12 Revise bars 1 - 4, and 5 - 8	Rollette: Dynamics	Play in groups of 3 like triplets	Think then play F scale	Sing scale; jump from note 1 to 4	Ex. 19

					Ex. 20
Day 4	Bars 13 - 16 Revise 1 - 4; 5 - 8; 9 - 12	Rollette: *Staccato*	Play in groups of 4	Write/learn F arpeggio Think/play F scale	Sing scale; jump from note 1 to 5
Day 5	Bars 17 - 21 Revise 13 -16	Record and listen critically	Play all notes at half speed with metronome	Name and finger F arpeggio Think/play F scale	Sing scale; jump from note 1 to 3	Finished
Day 6	Bars 22 - 24 Revise bars 13 - 21	Play Noughts and Crosses - any item from list	Play all notes at one speed faster	Think then play F arpeggio Think/play F scale	Sing scale; jump from note 1 to 4
Day 7	Play all through	Rollette	Increase metronome by one speed	Think then play F arpeggio Think/play F scale	Sing scale; jump from note 1 to 5
Comments					

With this system:

- You spend as long, or as short a time practising as you need. You see, it is not about getting the job done, but rather about the results you will achieve.
- You will only need to spend as long practising as it takes you to cover the tasks set for the day.
- You are not always starting from the beginning of the piece, and practising the start. You are constantly moving forward.
- You will not spend all your time polishing up just one bit of the music and ignoring the rest.
- You will not have just skimmed through the piece.
- You will have achieved a deep sense of satisfaction that you can play this music well, and you will make good progress.

Good practice can earn you rewards too.

Weekly planner plus rewards day:

This planner is constructed in a similar way to the weekly planner, but this one has a day off as a reward for keeping on track with your practice. So this needs to have the items from your skyscraper list on days 1 and 2 then a checkpoint. Your responsible adult will check to see if you have mastered the jobs so far.

Practice Checks:

Your parent, or other responsible adult, needs to check how you are doing before you can move on. You need to be able to demonstrate to this pretend teacher that you have mastered the items on your planner, even if it takes a couple of goes. If your 'teacher' agrees that you are on track, then you can have **the next day off**.

The next day that you practise you will move on to the next item on your skyscraper list. However, if your 'teacher' does not feel you have completed the tasks satisfactorily then you will have to revise how you are working and practise on day 3 too, since you will still need to complete the list of jobs before your next lesson.

You have another practice check, before your next lesson. This should show you how ready you are to present your work to your teacher.

Notice that you still have two days spare should you need them, to either finish off the work or apply some pressure games to make sure the music will stand up to being played to someone else.

When working with the Rewards Day planner you might not finish all the tasks. In this case you will need to talk to your teacher about reducing the amount of work to be practised during the week. After all, it would be better to have less work that can be done really well than so much work that you get put off doing anything at all!

(See the chapter called Quality not Quantity for some games to try to make your piece reliable.)

See the next page for the **Weekly planner plus rewards day.** Note that there are blank planners for you to use at the end of the book that you can photocopy.

The Weekly Planner Plus Rewards Day

Date	Lesson Time					
	Piece 1	**Piece 2**	**Piece 3**	**Scales**	**Aural**	**Theory**
	First page of **Mozart Flute Sonata** **Tools:** Skyscraper: all floor levels	Tidy up **Study 17:** slurs, *staccati* and dynamics **Tools:** Rollette	**Rondeau** Quavers must be accurate and even **Tools:** Distorted rhythms	Learn **F major** scale and arpeggio	Sing 5 notes of scale	Exercises 17 - 20
Day 1	Bars 1 - 4	Make a list of jobs and play Rollette	Play long/ short pattern	Write and learn notes of scale	Sing up and down 5 notes	Ex. 17
Day 2	Bars 5 - 8 Revise bars 1 - 4	Rollette: Slurs	Play short/long pattern	Name notes and finger scale	Sing scale; jump from note 1 to 3	Ex. 18
Day 3 DAY OFF	Must be able to play accurately, slowly, gaps are fine			Must be able to say letter names of F scale		
Day 4	Bars 9 - 12 Revise bars 1 - 4 and 5 - 8	Rollette: *Staccato*	Play in groups of 3 like triplets	Think and play F scale	Sing scale; jump from note 1 to 4	Ex. 19

Day						
Day 5	Bars 17 - 21 Revise bars 13 - 16	Record and listen critically	Play all notes in groups of 4	Name and finger F arpeggio Think and play F scale	Sing scale; jump from note 1 to 3	Ex. 20
Day 6 DAY OFF	Must be able to play from beginning to bar 16 - no stopping	Play Noughts and Crosses - any item from list		Must be able to say all letter names of scale and arpeggio		
Day 7	Bars 17 - 21 Revise bars 13 - 21	Go over any item from recording	Play all notes with slow metronome	Think then play F arpeggio Think and play F scale	Sing scale; jump from note 1 to 5	
Comments						

So, now you have a plan of campaign to build your skyscraper, and you have some realistic way of working on your pieces. It is not enough to vaguely know how the music goes, and skim over the notes and ideas like a butterfly, as beautiful as this image may be. Music is about communicating emotion, not just playing the notes reasonably well and getting from the beginning to the end without too much problem.

Getting a tick on the page should involve more than just playing some notes. It should be fluent, up to a decent speed, with dynamics, articulation, tone and expressing the character of the piece.

The checkpoint idea doesn't just stop with weekly planning. It is the most amazing thing, but time undergoes a change when we are faced with a Big Day. One day, say four months ago, you agreed to work towards an exam. Over the next few weeks you plodded along, messing around with scales pretending to be learning them, and playing through the pieces and then suddenly, you get the exam date for three or four weeks away, and panic sets in. You try to do everything you've have been told to do, but really you are only seriously working on it now, and so you don't really get on top of the tricky bits and you don't really know your scales. Time has flown!

The next thing that happens is that your parents step in, television programmes get banned, threats or bribes are made, tears are shed - basically, desperate measures are taken.

Let's change this scheme and rather than this panic-stricken approach, take the pressure off to enable us to play from memory, with confidence, assurance, and expression.

Planning helps you develop from week to week, but also will aid you as you work towards a goal such as an exam or a concert. Let's prepare for a **Big Day** next.

You will need a **Deadline** planner.

I have drawn up a blank planner at the back of the book for you to photocopy. You could colour in the sections with your favourite pens.

You will need to ask your teacher to help you to fill in the details, but the idea behind this chart is that you should divide up the work you have got to do into equal amounts across the number of available weeks. It is the same process as the daily planner, but on a larger scale. It helps you focus on the task ahead and makes you appreciate what you need to do to achieve it in a steady progression.

The practice checks will help you to organise your work well, so that you don't leave everything until the last minute.

Date	1 week from now must be able to play:	First piece slowly. One scale off by heart.
	2 weeks from now must be able to play:	Second piece slowly. First piece at half tempo. Two scales off by heart.
	3 weeks from now must be able to play:	All of the third piece. The second piece at half speed. The first piece at three-quarters speed. Three scales off by heart.
	4 weeks from now must be able to play:	All of third piece slowly. Second piece at three-quarters speed. First piece at correct tempo. Half required number of scales off by heart
	5 weeks from now must be able to play:	Third piece at half speed. Second piece at correct tempo. First piece with correct dynamics and tempo. Three-quarters of required number of scales off by heart.

	6 weeks from now must be able to play:	All pieces at correct tempo. Second piece with correct dynamics and tempo. First piece with correct articulation, phrasing, dynamics and tempo. Almost all required scales off by heart.
	7 weeks from now:	All pieces learned, fingered correctly. Dynamics, phrasing and articulation worked out. All scales learned off by heart.
	8 weeks from now:	All pieces to be played accurately with dynamics, articulation and phrasing. All scales off by heart.
	9 weeks from now:	Scales test
	10 weeks from now:	Record all pieces
	11 weeks from now:	Mock performance
	12 weeks from now:	**BIG DAY**

To Summarise:

Use your weekly planner to see:

- The actual tasks you need to do.
- The practice tools you will need.
- How to tell when you have finished your tasks.

Chapter 14

Expressive Playing

For some examinations in the UK, the pupil is asked about the piece of music: what period of musical history does it come from? Who else in that era might have composed a piece like this one? Importantly, what style is it in, and what exactly happens in the music in terms of dynamics, tempo, articulation and tonality?

Don't wait until you have an exam coming up before you start thinking in this way. You can do it from the very first time you play the piece.

This chapter is about trying to make your piece your own, an effective and expressive interpretation of the music.

It's a strange tradition that music teachers put circles round things – wrong notes, dynamics etc. The more you overlook things, the more circles you get on your page! I suppose the idea is that you will see the circles and realise that you have something to fix. You can get half a dozen circles on a page, and then these are supposed to stand out and shout at you to be noticed.

This may work if you are still using the music, but means absolutely nothing if you have learnt that section off by heart.

There is one problem here…the teacher shouldn't be doing the marks – *you* should. What the teacher should be saying to you is that you should study the score carefully at home and create those marks FOR

YOURSELF. The teacher should look at the prepared score at the next lesson, and try to find even one detail that you *haven't* marked. (The dreaded pencil can still be used for marking wrong notes though.)

However, you need to mark things in such a way so that:

Firstly:

You will see them and recognise them for what they are. For example, all dynamics should be circled, but all tempo marks need a box; articulation details, such as slurs, or *staccati*, could have a triangle around them.

Secondly:

Colour code all the dynamics with circles in different shades for different volume levels. You could use dark green for *pp*, a lighter shade for *p*; *mf* could be orange while *f* could be red.

In a similar way you would colour code the tempo boxes, although you need to try to use colours you haven't already used in the dynamics colour code.

You might be horrified at the thought of marking up your book like this, but if a little pink colour helps you remember the slurs in bar 5, then it has helped, and looks fun too.

(You can always make a copy of the music, as long as you mark it clearly 'for student's use'. The downside of this is that you cannot take a photocopy into an exam room so you will not be able to have your markings with you.)

Thirdly:

When playing from memory, then you might like to try this:

- Blink once for anything that was marked in green.
- Pause every time you get to anything that you marked as purple.
- Raise an eyebrow every time you had a triangle...and so on.

Not only do you have a very funky page of music but also you might notice that there is a pattern to the markings. With the colour system, you will be able to see the way the music is shaped, like a map of the area you are playing.

Story-Telling:

The colours not only make it easy to see the map, but you can also tell yourself a story as you play. You can make up a tale that will help you not only imagine why the dynamics are there in the first place, but also where they lead you. For example, a woodwind student of mine had a modern piece of music that she had worked through in detail but it was lacking in warmth, direction and enthusiasm. Even with all the colour markings on her music, her playing still lacked something.

I had a recording of this piece, and as we listened to it, I suggested that the opening was calm and untroubled, sunny and feeling like a morning in the holidays, but then a dark cloud came but that was fine as the sun came out again after that. The clouds gathered again. A cat crept round the garden and spied a bird in a tree. The cat slunk up to the tree and the bird twittered and flew away in a panic. The clouds disappeared and the ending returned to the tranquil summer's day.

Well, on her next play-through, there was a transformation. The music had an element of fun and lightness, then darkness (and sadness, because the sunny day changed to a gloomy one). There were silky slurs where the cat crept up, with light *staccati* where the bird section was. So, as you can see, she had used the story to help make sense of what the markings had told her but she confessed that she hadn't really thought about the dynamics and articulation, just how the story went.

Minimalist Markings:

Now, this is fine if there are a lot of markings for you to consider but there are some pieces of music with minimal information about dynamics and articulation. There are quite a number of Baroque sonatas for woodwind like this.

You will need to experiment.

You will need to make a list of possible questions, for instance, if you feel the music might need a *rubato*, then where will it start? How slow will it go? Does it even *need* a *rubato* here? How about speeding it up? How should the dynamics vary? Baroque tongued notes are often clear and slightly detached, but should they all be like that?

You are going to rate the answers only on how convincing you feel the music is. The more answers you give to the question, the more confident you will be of your solution.

Don't be afraid to test ideas out.

To Summarise:

> * Mark up your music in colours for each element.
> * Make a map of how the music goes.
> * Tell yourself a story to describe what happens in the music.

Congratulations on reading about better practising. Make sure that you try some of the ideas, especially the skyscraper building tasks and the games. Please read Part 2: *Let's Perform*, for ideas on how to prepare for the day when you perform your music in public.

A Practice Checklist

Are you standing or sitting well? Check by looking in a mirror.

Always aim for your best possible sound.

If you are a piano player, make sure your fingers really press the keys like you would push your fingers into sand. Play with a good touch and even volume.

Listen carefully and critically to what you play.

If you make a mistake, put a spot over it on your music and be sure to go over and over that bit in your practice session, but don't go back to the beginning and have another run at the piece, and don't go back and go even faster at it...you will just arrive at the mistake again even sooner and still not have fixed the problem!

Check that you are observing the markings on the music: slurs, dynamics etc.

Is the rhythm correct? Get out your metronome and check it!

Practise SLOWLY especially at first. If you practise so slowly you don't make a mistake, you have practised perfectly!

Occasionally pretend you are performing the piece...no stopping come what may.

Are you thinking about the character of the piece? If it is supposed to be light and bouncy, are you playing it like that? For more information on this have a look at the chapter on Expressive Playing.

Always imagine your music without your instruments...can you remember the fingerings, how the music starts, and what volume it should be?

Part 2

Let's Perform

If you can imagine it, you can achieve it.

If you can dream it, you can become it.

William Arthur Ward

Introduction

If you have managed to try out most of the ideas in the first part of this book then you will be so well set up for future performances that you probably will never get really troubled by stage-fright and performance anxiety. You now have a confident, secure product that you can feel proud of and that will stand up under pressure. You can justifiably feel satisfied with your efforts.

You can walk onto that stage with your head held high and an inner smile because, as a well-known advertisement on the television says, "You're worth it!"

Experts have estimated that of all the things we worry about 40% will never happen, 30% are past (and all the worry in the world can't change them), 12% are needless worries about our health, 10% are petty, miscellaneous worries, leaving 8% for things that legitimately deserve our concern and thoughts.

With the techniques in this book you can change the 40% anxieties so that you can feel confident and anxiety free, the 30% worries by altering the way you perceive them, and attack the 8% ones so that you can feel calm, relaxed and confident and look forward to your next performance or exam.

Once we understand why we get anxious about music tests and exams we can do several things to help ourselves:

- Change our thoughts and beliefs.
- Let go of the past and move forward.
- Develop positive feeling about ourselves.
- Develop feelings of control and confidence.

Learning music is a difficult enough task in most cases, but, by going this extra mile and using thoughts generated from within your mind, you can gain control over both the music and yourself.

Chapter 15

Emotional Preparation and Performance Anxiety

"Anxiety is the gap between the now and the future."

Fritz Perls

Performing is the live communication of music. We go to music concerts because we want to be immersed in music. We perform because we love music, want to express it and share it. But how much do we actually enjoy the occasion?

Nerves and butterflies in the tummy are all part of the way our bodies react when doing something in front of others. Indeed, our bodies have evolved to anticipate what might happen in the future. Any unknown and possibly worrying situation may need us to decide whether to flee from a danger or to stand and fight it.

For most of us, the performing occasion produces anxiety in any degree from a little excited to completely fearful. We find ourselves in a state of fear whereby, from a physiological perspective, we freeze with fright but experience a rush of adrenalin, which goes to the vital organs to prepare us for fight or flight. Now this was helpful for our ancestors who, when faced with a woolly mammoth, needed to decide whether to flee from it or fight it but which, in the twenty-first century is really rather unhelpful.

Stage fright, or performance anxiety.

This usually strikes as the musician goes on stage and begins her/his performance. They get it when being judged in competitions and even when doing recordings or broadcasts. Some get it in rehearsals when they might have a section that they play solo and can even get it when they are within earshot of others when they are practising.

Thus, this anxiety is associated with being listened to, being criticised and being looked at. The cause of this distress was discussed in *Mind Over Matter*, but briefly, fright mimics the 'flight or fight' reflex in the body, resulting in the body making a chemical called adrenalin and consequently produces all the typical features of preparing the body for action.

Some of the effects of too much adrenalin can be:

- Difficulty in breathing.
- A rapid pulse.
- Dry mouth.
- Sweaty hands.
- Loss of fine motor control: fingers tremble and feel clumsy.
- Inability to see or hear clearly.
- An inability to think clearly or we go blank and 'stupid'.
- Tension.
- Stiff body movements.
- Dizziness.
- Nausea.
- Feeling unable to be expressive.

Any performer will tell you that such changes to the body are often completely inappropriate, for example sweaty fingers on flute keys or bows bouncing. This incorrect form of excitement turns into panic when no natural outcome can be achieved since you probably do not expect to fight the examiner or flee for your life.

Too much adrenalin in the body gives a situation akin to an animal finding its escape barred and becoming confused. It suffers a state where its flight has been aborted and it experiences loss of breath and extreme shaking. It is this state that is most typical of the performer struck by stage-fright in the centre of the stage like an animal caught in a car's headlights.

The presence of anxiety in the musician produces a range of behaviour that is unhelpful and inhibits our ability to function on top form. Performance anxiety occurs when we are concerned about the quality of performance. It is a self-conscious, self-doubting awareness that hinders performance instead of helping. We worry that people are looking at us and that we may lose control or make a fool of ourselves.

These issues all involve heightened anxiety. In overcoming them, the goal is not to get rid of anxiety because it is normal; it is part of being human. Anxiety helps ready us for action and is there for our survival. Pre-performance butterflies in the tummy may be unpleasant but they *can* often give an important edge to a performance. Some players hover around the fringes of anxiety, but it is when we cannot make the switch from anxiety to excitement that the problems begin.

Fear, anxiety or worry is a mental response to a perceived danger or threat. Fear releases chemical hormones that can inhibit performance and shut you down. You want to curl up and make yourself as small as possible. When you are afraid in an exam then you look small. Your shoulders hunch and tense up so that they almost meet your ears. Because you are looking small you also play small. You don't take risks with dynamics. You focus on the negative and you worry about making mistakes.

Fear is a bit like the Wizard in the magical Land of Oz. It is an unseen presence, a booming voice behind a curtain. Fear is as big and as powerful as we imagine it to be. Musicians may resist fear, try to deny it or attempt to conquer it. So what is the best way of defeating fear?

Actually, the best solution is *none of these things* – not resisting fear, not denying it and not trying to conquer it. Fear is a natural part of performance. If you're not a bit scared then you are probably in trouble. When you resist fear you are only keeping it alive. Accept it and recognise that your body is telling you to become energised. Don't let fear scare you. Feel the fear and play anyway.

Courage is not the absence of fear, but acting despite being fearful. So, if you are feeling anxious and nervous and yet still step onto that stage or enter that exam room, then you are very courageous.

It is possible to experience performance anxiety without it leading to panic and choking.

Choking is the term the sport's world gives to a situation when an athlete is unable to manage anxiety and fear at crucial times during sports events. Although anxiety is usually the central cause of choking, other negative feelings can also fuel this feeling. When you feel tense, your muscles tighten up and can cause you to lose the keen sense of touch and fine motor control so necessary for musicians.

One of these negative feelings centres around the fact that you don't think you are good enough to succeed. This is not to do with how well you play your music, but your overall sense of who you are. You, in fact, sabotage yourself by doubting how acceptable you are. Don't be afraid of choking. **Breathe** and **focus** instead.

Breathing and focussing:

It is natural that, when trying hard and focussing well, we hold our breath. But oxygen is energy. It helps muscles to relax and clears the mind. When you hold your breath, you are creating pressure and a nervous feeling. Musicians who choke start to become nervous about being nervous. To break this cycle you need to learn to breathe well.

The pattern of your breathing affects the pattern of your performance. When you are anxious, deep breathing helps bring your mind and body back to a state of calm.

> Try breathing in through your nose while you count to five and breathe out through your mouth as though you are blowing a feather in the air while you count to seven. Keep your shoulders still and use your tummy muscles to breathe with, to make this really effective.

Anxiety is a result of negative self-talk that often distracts the mind from focussing on the problem at hand. For example, when pupils become worried about their music exam they may repeatedly tell themselves that they are going to mess up, or that they can't remember the music at all, or the examiner is going to judge them rather than listen to the music. This type of thinking interferes with focussing on the exam.

Imagine dropping a stone into a large lake. The stone (performance situation) hitting the water causes ripples (a thought) which, if unchallenged because you are comfortable with the situation, allows the ripples to find their natural plane and the water becomes calm again.

However, if you are uncomfortable, then you begin to erect a barrier that bounces the ripples back on themselves, causing internal chaos. It is vital to learn ways of breaking down these self-erected barriers so that you can go on to become a good performer. A musician is most likely to feel anxious when their attention is stuck on the consequences of going wrong or making a mistake, rather than being completely absorbed in the performance of the music.

Part of the nervous system that plays an important part in our emotional life is called the *autonomic nervous* system. Its function is to arouse the body for the kind of responses needed for fear and anxiety, in other words, running from danger or preparing for fighting.

Some of the effects you notice when this system is activated are:

- Dilation of the pupils.
- Opening the eyelids.
- Stimulation of the sweat glands.
- Opening up of the blood vessels in large muscles.
- Closing down of blood vessels in the rest of the body.
- Increase in heart rate.
- Opening up of the bronchial tubes in the lungs.
- Slowing down of the secretions in the digestive system.

Effects many a nervous musician knows only too well are:

- Little or no saliva produced.
- All or nothing thinking such as, "That's it, I've made a mistake, now I've failed!"
- Tense muscles.
- Rapid breathing.

So to stop the panicky emotion you need to:

- Encourage saliva production... try chewing some gum.
- It is very hard to make adrenalin if you have had a good meal, so don't starve yourself before a concert or performance.
- Ignore 'all or nothing' thoughts... try saying to yourself, "It was only a slip, I'm doing all right."
- Relax your muscles... try some of the techniques in Chapter 3 or read *Mind Over Matter.*
- Deliberately breathe in a relaxed way. Take deep breaths and let the adrenalin kick you into full awareness of who you are, where you are and what you are about to do.
- Learn to relax.

Relaxation:

Relaxation is a good technique to learn. It is a skill that you will benefit from throughout your life. The more you practise this the better you will become at releasing tension.

Find a quiet place in your mind:

Close your eyes, and with every out breath count from 10 to 1.

When you reach 1 imagine that you can see a door.

Open the door and walk through to where you can create a unique place of relaxation. For example, if you like to be at a beach, then create the beach and find a nice spot to sit or lie.

Notice the sun in the sky and how the gentle air brushes past your cheeks, and warms your skin.

Notice how the sea sounds as the waves break on the shore and the sound as the sea sucks back before the next wave. Feel the comforting sand in your hands and how it feels on your feet. Notice the clouds floating in the sky just being blown gently on the breeze.

Hear the birds in the sky and enjoy their songs and chirps; how they love to perform without fear or self-awareness. Become engrossed in the scene and examine your goals as you experience the beach.

Take your time here.

In this state of relaxation you can imagine your future performance, how you will play with beauty and serenity.

Visualise the event, the way you enter the exam room or stage; imagine the music as you play it in your mind; imagine how beautifully you interpret the music.

Give yourself permission to make mistakes, but flow through the music despite them. Imagine the way the audience cheers and claps.

When you have enjoyed how your music has flowed and how 'in the zone' you were, count down from 10 to 1 to come back out.

Relaxing deeply like this calms both the mind and the body. This process takes time to really become effective, but even after only a few days you will become better at it. You could try a slight variation on this relaxation by:

- Sitting quietly.
- Breathing gently and slowly.
- Focussing on your breathing.
- On every out breath you repeat a word like 'calm' or 'relax'.

Chapter 16

Talking to Yourself

A child that receives care, approval and encouragement from its primary caregivers receives positive messages about himself such as, "you matter as a person," or "you can succeed." Unfortunately, infants may misunderstand even the most positive and loving of responses to their cries. They may be crying because they are experiencing a feeling of fear and they are rewarded with a nappy change. They could be hungry but get put to bed instead; neither response to the infant is unloving or unkind but inappropriate as far as the infant is concerned.

From a psychological point of view, performance anxiety can cause us to key into our 'inner child'. As you experience any emotion you cannot help but be transported back into your past when you had the same emotion. When did you have this fear? When you were an infant! You may have been hungry, thirsty or in pain but as an infant, you were absolutely unable to do anything about it by yourself, except cry. That cry expressed how you felt at that time. Your parents may have thought you were just crying, but you may have been expressing terror and hopelessness. So, the feelings of anxiety experienced in this genuinely anxious time of preparing for performance slips you back in time to those infantile and early childhood emotions. This reaction to your memories is called your 'inner child'.

Negative Self-Talk:

As children, we believe what we are told about ourselves. If one or both of our primary caregivers was critical of us, by saying how clumsy we were or how hopeless we were, or even just ignored us, we probably took over the task of criticising ourselves from them as we got older. Also, teachers, relatives and our peers can contribute to making us feel 'bad' about ourselves.

So, negative self-talk is something we have learnt to do over the years. After all, we were not born with negative thoughts. When you were a baby, I don't suppose that you thought how messy your hair was, or whether your arms were fat.

Negative self-talk is usually a mixture of half-truths, poor logic and an unbalanced focus on a problem. Although all this seems self-defeating, in fact it serves a purpose. It protects us from potentially uncomfortable situations. Mostly, however, it gets in the way of our dreams and potential.

There is a little voice inside your head that chatters on, explaining and exploring, asking questions and answering itself, providing a running commentary on what you are doing, experiencing and feeling. It is automatic and unstoppable and often self-defeating.

Nobody would be allowed to speak to you the way you speak to yourself. If your performance falls short of perfect, you see yourself as a total failure, and you say, "I've made a mistake, that's so typical of me!" "I'm such an idiot" or "I am so pathetic."

Your internal voice can give you encouragement and support one moment but make you uncertain and nervous the next. You are your own severest critic. Your internal voice gives you a harder time than any external person. Who else can get away with saying, "You look dreadful today," or "stupid fool, you've gone and done it again!" Who else hammers away at you with cruel comments about how you messed up your exam pieces, or how you tripped over the steps onto the stage when everyone was looking?

An examiner or audience can get cast into the role of 'parent' and so the exam candidate can have a disproportionate need for their approval and fear of their criticism. It is as if your very life depends on how these adults respond to you. Like the helpless infant, you can feel as if you are falling apart or about to drop into a bottomless pit that has opened up within yourself. You could spend the whole concert or exam feeling that you are being judged and found wanting, and wishing you were somewhere else.

Your inner voice is sounding very negative.

As musicians we often find that we are happily playing our piece of music in a concert or an exam when the little voice in our head draws attention to some difficult bars coming up. Our focus is then diverted away from the piece and turns into a thought or a slight anxiety. We then lose the freedom of performance and concentrate instead on any tightening of our stomach or dryness of our mouth. So in order to ignore this inner voice you need to learn to control it.

To change the voice, try this experiment:

Change the voice:

- Try reading the last two paragraphs in your mind and listen to that little voice.
- Slow down that internal voice.
- Now try speeding it up.
- Try changing the sound of that voice to a silly voice like Mickey Mouse.
- Remember a time when someone made a comment to you that you didn't like.
- Now speed up that voice and make it sound silly.

That voice doesn't seem so bad now, does it? How silly some of the things you say to yourself can sound!

Internal voice – Positive self-talk:

Now you are going to make that internal voice work for you instead of against you. You can turn those negative comments into positive ones that reassure and comfort you.

Close your eyes for a minute or two, and imagine there is a friendly mirror in front of you.

Look at yourself in it, and imagine someone who loves or deeply appreciates you standing next to you.

Hear all the lovely things they say about you, feel how much they love you. Give them time to tell you all about how wonderful they think you are, how wonderfully you play and how proud they are of you for doing this performance.

Now open your eyes and go and look in a proper mirror.

Look at yourself eyeball to eyeball, and hear all that again inside your head.

Put these thoughts where your old internal voice was. Hear again all those lovely things you heard: feel all that love and respect. Let it flood over you and let those really good feelings soak into your very being.

Tell yourself, in your new confident internal voice, positive things like, "I am very relaxed...I am very confident...I enjoy playing my music...I can play with real flow..."

Try doing this daily, and your inner voice will cease being your critic and instead will become your best friend, helping you to become more confident about yourself very quickly.

Let me give you an example:

It was exam day. A grade five flautist was feeling almost sick with fear and was not only as white as a sheet, but was trembling, breathing fast and sweating. She had a glass of water with her because she had a dry mouth, and which she could barely put down on the table in the exam room because she was shaking so much. She did not look at the examiner as she came into the room. She almost crept in, looking as though she wished she were anywhere but in that room.

The examiner's reaction was extremely interesting. He looked at the girl and immediately looked worried, and sat on the edge of his chair. He didn't know whether or not to try to get her to look at him, and so shuffled papers on his desk whilst waiting for her to reply to his question about what pieces she would be playing. He looked stiff and uneasy. The flautist's inner child was working overtime, as was the examiner's inner parent.

Picture the same scenario a couple of years later after some good work on her performance anxiety. It was grade seven exam day. The same flautist walked into the exam room with a slight smile on her face, looked at the examiner and greeted him politely. She was breathing slowly and carefully, and had been chewing some gum prior to entering the exam room to stop her mouth from drying up. She put the examiner at his ease, and he sat back into his chair, looking relaxed and excited about what this pupil was going to play. She was obviously in charge of herself, and the music, and confident that she could cope with whatever might happen during the performance.

This example is absolutely true.

What had happened in between those two events for this young person? Well, we strengthened her ability to cope with both mental and physical aspects of performance using many of the techniques in this book, but we also worked on her self-talk.

Just as parents are expected to bring up their child to independence, so the music teacher's role is to help the pupil develop musical independence through warmth, encouragement, positive regard, suitable praise, and careful criticism. The teacher's role is as much about building up your inner child as it is about training you in the art of musicianship. With a strong inner child we feel ourselves cared for, supported, encouraged. We feel certain that any slips or errors in our playing are just what they should be – minor glitches: "Wrong note there, never mind!"

Strangely enough, it is girls and women who tend to need a strong inner carer, since they need to feel safe and secure before they can open up and express themselves to others, whereas boys and men seem to see performance more in terms of doing rather than being. They seem to expect to have to go out and prove themselves because it is in this way that they gain admiration and approval.

Inner Child and Inner Critic:

You need an inner critic to help you be alert to the quality of your work and aware of things that need to be worked on in your music, but it needs to be balanced by the inner carer who creates warm support and keeps negative feelings in check. You need to worry about being neither approved nor disapproved of, but be comfortable just being yourself NOW. Forget the past. Don't worry about the future. Just enjoy what you are doing here and now.

Curiously, the audience or examiner also has an inner child and can cast the student as the inner parent! You would find this hard to believe, but examiners want you to take charge; they want you not to allow any slips to spoil the music so they can relax, listen and enjoy the music.

Chapter 17

Learning to Deal With Failure

The first thing to remember is that making mistakes is simply part of the way we learn. If you are learning to skateboard you will certainly discover that you were not born able to do it. You fall off and have to start again. You learn control and balance through practice. Falling off is not a catastrophe; it may make you feel silly, but it isn't life threatening. Remember, you were not born able to play the harp or the accordion. For some reason, musicians are expected to be perfect whereas they need to be trained to accomplish something that is as close to perfection as possible.

Modern music recordings don't help. We listen to our favourite artist and we hear a perfect track. What we don't hear are the many other attempts that were recorded. Also we don't know all the tweaks and corrections the sound engineer made before releasing the final recording. When you go to a live concert, you can hear the clarinettist breathing, or the brass player playing an odd note. It isn't faultless. In real life and in real music, things don't always go perfectly.

Mistakes happen. They are part of life. It is what we do about our mistakes that mark us out as high quality musicians.

Self-confidence:

Practice is the key not only to improving our playing ability but also to self-confidence. Those who attempt to perform without knowing their pieces well are tempting fate and don't deserve to feel confident. Practice is a time when we are particularly *conscious* of what we are doing. Performance, on the other hand, can be more *trance-like* in quality because we no longer need to focus intently on what we are doing or how we are doing it.

We have already dealt with the things we are trying to accomplish through practice:

1. We have worked a great deal on technical variables so they can be constantly reproduced correctly and dependably. We have worked through weaknesses to eliminate vulnerable parts in our music.

2. We have developed confidence through playing passages several times correctly so that our playing becomes more 'automatic' and all details are correctly rehearsed.

3. We have practised several variations on a piece, so allowing the choice of how to play the piece and make it our own.

4. We have worked hard.

The goal of practice is to eliminate stress. Once you can get into this stress-free environment you can be in the 'zone', where all details are correct and all details dovetail into a spontaneous flow of inspiration.

Do not be afraid of 'failure', like wrong notes in your concert piece. The capacity to keep failures in perspective, to accept them and go forward to greater things is one of the key qualities in winners, whether in music, sport or life.

Athletes use sports psychology to help them achieve their successes. We are going to use some of their ideas to help break away from the 'what if' mentality that we so easily get when we have a tricky bit, or just any bit, in our music we are worried about.

Athletes often watch videos of themselves in action. They will play the tape slowly, going forwards and backwards over the section they are interested in. They can spot their mistakes and learn from them in this way. You also see them mentally rehearsing their run or their rowing even before the race has started, by doing it in slow motion.

For the musician, memories of past performances, when things went wrong and we felt we had let ourselves down, linger on and spoil these action replays. So first we need to deal with the past and get it out of our heads.

Unpleasant Memories:

Sometimes we have unpleasant memories of:

- A time when we played badly.
- A time when one or more musical disasters happened in a performing situation.

We felt criticised by others, including our own inner critic, of our poor standard.

Such memories may be few or many, recent or back in the past. Since nobody is born with the ability to play, we have had to learn as much by our mistakes as by our correct playing. Regrettably, when mistakes are made in public, then the memory of them is so much harder to remove. It is possible though.

There are some steps towards dealing with this:

- Accept that mistakes are part of the process of learning.
- Accept that critical people exist out there, and don't be concerned about what they say. (Easier said than done!)
- Be honest about your present standard of performance and musicianship and get to work on things left undone.
- Deal with stage fright to eliminate or neutralise the memories of unpleasant performing situations.

So, let's deal with unpleasant past memories:

1. Our past experiences of 'bad' performances stay in our memories. They usually are bright, colourful and painful.
2. Remember what happened in all its intensity: big, bright, close to you, and feel the pain and emotion that went with it.
3. Now make your memory go black and white, make it go smaller and smaller until it's about the size of a postage stamp, dark and black and white.
4. Make any voice associated with this memory speed up until it sounds fast and silly.
5. Make the memory get smaller and smaller and, in your internal eye, move it up and off to the left.

Do this for each memory and you will soon be able to think about the past without the painful emotion.

Giving yourself permission to fail frees you up to accomplish the task at hand. For instance:

- Choose a task you have been doing under pressure. It could be slurring the upper notes in the top flute register, an exposed entry, or breathing fast and deep enough for to play that group of semiquavers in that piece of Mozart.
- Now, give yourself permission to fail and then play it. If you get it right this time, keep doing it until you *do* fail.

How many goes did you have before you went wrong? Did you find it hard to fail? Did you have to try hard to go wrong? Did you find that when you stopped trying, you started to succeed?

Chapter 18

Trying and Trusting

Learning to accept failure makes it sound like you are going to be losing the power over your music making. You want to be in control and aware of your playing. You expect that the harder you try the better the results will be. This may be one way of playing, but it tenses the muscles and occupies the mind, allowing that inner critic to appear on the scene. Sports people often find that the harder they try, the worse they perform. This was seen very clearly in the Olympic Games 2008 where relay runners tried so hard to hand the baton over to the next runner that they dropped it and were disqualified.

The disadvantages of trying:

- Trying causes muscles to tense, losing those delicate finger movements needed by musicians.
- Trying causes panic.
- Trying causes your mind to go blank and you can't remember the fingering of a simple note, or understand the very first page of your exam piece.
- Trying is the opposite of what we need in a performance. At this stage, when we are ready to perform in some sort of public way, we should be trusting ourselves: *doing* without *trying*.
- Trying is a form of desire similar to envy, ambition and other forms of self-fulfilment, which, when you are about to perform,

will not be helpful. To let the examiner know how hard you are trying is defensive and not reassuring.

- Trying is allied to 'force' and 'strain' and assumes difficulty. For example, we hear the expressions "you must try harder" and "if at first you don't succeed try, try, try again."

Trying harder and harder:

As we have already discovered, in *Let's Practise*, tricky bits and the like do not respond to simply trying again and again. Indeed, the harder we try, the more we seem to fail. Why is it that our minds go blank at the beginning of the exam? It is because we are trying too hard. We try in an anxious and frustrated kind of way and this makes us tense up. This kind of trying comes from a fear that we maybe aren't good enough and we doubt ourselves. If we didn't doubt our ability to perform the task, we wouldn't need to try. You could probably play *Happy Birthday* to yourself at home, but if you had to play it at *The Last Night of the Proms* in front of an audience of thousands then you might well start to become self-conscious and doubt yourself.

Even in lessons, we want to show our teacher how well we have practised. We, therefore, try hard. We are probably more tense than usual and thus things don't go as well as we would like. So, we try harder, and guess what, things actually go worse than before. We get more tense and doubtful about our playing.

Candidates try hard in their exams and end up feeling tense and under strain. Often they are disappointed with their efforts. (Maybe the answer is to think of their exam as just like having a lesson, and that it doesn't really matter how well they do. However, it may have the effect of reducing their motivation to perform well. They may not put enough *effort* into their playing.)

> "Trying fails, awareness cures."
>
> Fritz Perls

Trust, on the other hand, allows you to be more relaxed. You have done the work. You know the pieces. You could play them blindfolded, standing on your head and in your sleep.

Physical trust is identical with economy of effort, since it is the correct use of muscles that is important. Trusting your body without the effort of trying, will allow you to enjoy feeling relaxed while you play. The more relaxed you are, the more control you will have, and still have some power in reserve.

Mental trust is about letting go and allowing your mind to do what it does best with the minimum of interference. The mind knows all those notes and finger movements and a great deal more. Subconscious powers can retrieve and formulate ideas that lie below the surface, even when asleep. Let self-doubt interfere as little as possible. Trust your memory and let it work for you.

The difficulty with trust is that is goes against so many of the ways in which we are taught to think. We believe we are functioning best when we are 'in control'. We force our brain to work hard and ignore the brain's ability to take care of itself. We think so hard that we become unaware of other information that may be of more use to us.

Past events:

Unfortunately, we also pick up a lack of trust from past events. If we felt sick with fear prior to our previous exam, we don't always trust ourselves that next exam time we will feel fine. If we fell up the steps onto the stage last time we performed, we don't trust ourselves not to do it this time. We do not see trust as a way out of our dilemma because we do not trust 'trust'.

Thoughts themselves are not a problem, but you could let these thoughts come and then actively make them go. To do this you need to choose relaxed concentration.

Relaxed Concentration:

Be aware of your body: how you are standing or sitting; how your arms feel; if there is any tension, let it go. Focus your attention on a single movement of your body while you are playing and notice how you can subtly shift to a more relaxed, and accurate, kind of moving.

'The obstacles to our trusting', writes Timothy Gallwey in *The Inner Game of Music* (Green and Gallwey, 1987) 'tend to cluster in three main areas':

1. Do you have problems with your **self-image**?
    Are you concerned about what your peers think of you?
    Are you concerned about what the audience or examiner thinks of your playing?
    Are you worried that you will fail?

2. Do you doubt your **control** of the situation?
    Do you feel stuck with an interpretation that feels flat or rigid?
    Are you unable to loosen up and play creatively?
    Are you uncomfortable about taking risks in your performances when in the spotlight?

3. Do you **doubt** your abilities?
    Are you worried that you aren't really musical?
    Do you suffer from performance anxiety?
    Do you doubt your ability to play under pressure?

This may not cover all your issues, but if you think about them, you will probably find they will fit into one of the above categories.

Don't be undermined by your fears and worries; trust your ability, your hard practice, your training and let go. Focus on something like the position of your bow, or the weight of your left arm, and just play.

We have seen that doubts and fears make us tense. Tension makes you feel that you need to try hard to stay focussed. There are two things that you can do about this:

1. Give yourself permission to fail:

How reassuring it is when you know you can have another go at something. Wouldn't it be nice if you knew that you could go into the exam room to play your pieces and play them again if they went wrong? Well, it is an amazing thing, but if you actually *try* to fail, you will find it hard to make any mistakes.

2. Find a simple task inside the complex one:

If you have a complicated run of fast notes, then see if you can find a smaller pattern within those notes, almost as if you have a whole sentence of notes that you could split into individual words. You will probably see that there is a pattern to those notes, and this will help you to play the pattern rather than focussing on the individual notes. By releasing your control over the tiny, individual portions of the music, you will be able to play with more trust and freedom as you see the bigger picture.

Chapter 19

Mental Preparation for Performance

> By thinking differently, you'll behave differently and get different results.

We tend to do what we think about most. If we think we play badly, then we will play badly. We may complain that we lack natural ability or talent, yet we *all* have talents and abilities. They may be different from other people's talents but we can get to see ours as being as good as anyone else's. If you decide on being as good as you can possibly be, then you can get what you want. You can create your own standard of excellence by *imagining* it.

The mind messes up more often than the body does. For example, take riding a bike. You are cycling along and you see an awkward corner and your mind says, "don't fall off", and guess what, you wobble and immediately come crashing down. One teacher was trying to avoid the winter 'flu so that she would be well enough to accompany her performers, so she was saying things like "I don't want to be ill," and what happened? Yes, you've guessed, she went down with 'flu about two days before the event!

The mind can only concentrate on one thing at a time, so the key to success is not to allow negative thoughts to intrude while playing. Even a neutral thought is better than being sabotaged by bad ones.

One way to introduce a neutral thought is to have one word or a short phrase that, when you think about it, gives you pleasure, makes you feel good, or reminds you of beautiful things. You could even be silly and try making up some nonsense words too, such as "wuggle," "shugshug" or "kerplickle." You could think about some strange things like what you are going to do at the weekend or who is going to win the Formula One Grand Prix.

The success cycle:

The success cycle is the relationship between how you feel about yourself and how you are likely to perform under pressure. If you are feeling positive about yourself and have a good self-image, then you are more likely to have a positive attitude, which in turn is likely to lead to higher expectations. This usually leads to improved practice (either more concentrated and focussed or longer practice sessions), and with the improvements the level of performance increases. Consequently, your self-image is enhanced and your performance spirals gently and positively upwards.

However, the effects of a negative self-image can be just as powerful and will move you downwards. We have so many negative thoughts in life.

Unfortunately we are surrounded by them:

- I don't want to slip on the ice.
- I don't want to be grounded.
- I don't want to look bad.
- I don't want to make a fool of myself.
- I don't want to play badly.
- I don't want to feel nervous.
- I don't want to mess up my performance again…etc!

Sometimes they come disguised as 'if only':

- If only I hadn't played so badly.
- If only that man in the audience hadn't coughed.
- If only I had spent more time practising my entry.
- If only I hadn't chosen that particular piece.

Sometimes they come in another guise altogether:

- I *want* to play well.
- I *want* to lose my stage fright.
- I *want* my hands to stop shaking.

This last list looks as if it should be positive, but really what you are saying is "last time I didn't play well but this time I will," or, "if only my hands didn't shake so much I would be in control of my flute playing and get a grip on myself." Do you see how it works?

We need to develop some mental toughness then, to get to grips with our thoughts and self-talk. There are six attributes of mental toughness which all begin with C.

The six Cs of Mental Toughness:

- **Confidence:**

Tiger Woods, the famous golfer, said, "Every time I play, in my own mind I'm the favourite." Confident musicians have a can-do attitude and a belief that they can handle anything that comes their way.

- **Control:**

Successful musicians are able to control their emotions and behaviour. They focus on what they can control but don't allow the things they can't be in command of to affect them.

- **Commitment:**

Mentally tough musicians focus their time and energy on their goals and dreams. They 'hunger' for success, and work hard to achieve it.

- **Composure:**

You need to be able to keep your cool, stay focussed and deal with any problems with a calm attitude when the heat is on.

- **Courage:**

You need to be prepared to take a risk. You can display courage even when feeling very fearful.

- **Consistency:**

Mentally tough musicians possess an inner strength. They often play their best when they feel at their worst. They don't make excuses. They don't blame other people for things that go wrong. You may not always be able to control what happens, but you can control how you respond to any slips or errors.

In order to improve, we need to recognise our strengths and weaknesses. We have to work on our pieces to get them free from errors since they will always stand out like a neon sign, and we have to work on our mental attitude too.

> The most important part of a musician's body is above their shoulders.
> Adapted from Ty Cobb

We are going to use the power of the mind to build mental toughness. We are going to imagine it.

Goal-setting:

We are going to use the power of your own mind to think about what you really want – your goals.

These following four points are important:

- Decide what you want.
- Do something.
- Notice what happens.
- Change what you do until you achieve your goal.

This list seems quite normal actually. Most of the time this is just how you go about getting to any of your own targets. Take wanting an *iPod*, for instance. You <u>decide</u> on the model and colour you want, and you decide to save up for it. You choose to <u>do something</u> to get the money, like saving up your pocket money and doing jobs. After a couple of weeks of effort you <u>notice what has happened</u>. You count up your money. You decide that you need to do more jobs and save all your money rather than buying sweets now and again. So you <u>change what you are doing</u> in order to get your *iPod*. When thinking in this positive way you will need to:

State your goal clearly and positively. For example, "I want to play my exam music well." Here, you will need to be careful that you don't actually say what you don't want: "Don't mess up like last time." If you are riding your bike and you think, "I hope I don't fall off," you can almost guarantee that you will. Or if you think Friday 13th is going to be a bad day, then it probably will be. Your mind is very powerful, so, to make your goal positive and clear you need to focus on what you *really* want.

Sit down and be quiet for a few minutes. Just close your eyes and imagine yourself playing really well. Imagine the exam room or concert hall. Imagine yourself walking in and beginning to play, noticing your fingers flying over the keys and being in total control. Imagine the audience clapping and cheering, and yourself bowing and smiling to them. Say something (in your mind or out loud) like, "I want to feel more confident in my playing and use my abilities to the full, especially at the exam or when I have to play in public."

What will you feel, hear and experience about your success when you have achieved this goal? Try to imagine what you will hear when you are playing, and when people are cheering and clapping. **Smile** gently and feel a warm glow deep inside you at this wonderful picture. **Say**, in your head or out loud, something like, "I will feel confident and walk tall. I will play with expression and confidence."

What you are going to do to achieve this? How do you see yourself doing it? What can you do about it immediately? Say something like this to yourself, "I will make sure I do my practice as well as I can."

Now open your eyes. Already your mind is feeling positive and excited about achieving your goal. You have strengthened your inner carer, too, by doing this exercise.

The Journey:

This technique is about the journey to your performance rather than the end product. You need to stay focussed on your goal and not allow yourself to get distracted. Keep your eye on the *iPod* and don't get sidetracked and buy CDs instead. You need to keep your motivation going and keep that fire alight to get where you want to be, and that is playing your amazing music with confidence, can-do attitude and belief in yourself.

> Whatever you think you are, you are always more than that.

If the advice above is too daunting, then think how your favourite person might go about being confident and mentally tough. This could be a pop singer or an actor, it doesn't matter who it is, but it needs to be someone that you wish you could be.

Role Model:

> Try choosing a role model for yourself. Choose someone that you would like to be. It doesn't have to be a musician.
>
> Imagine your role model playing your music; see and feel what it is like for her/him to be doing that task or using that skill. Get the sense of what it is like for your role model to be playing your music.
>
> Close your eyes and just pretend to be your role model. Imagine what it is like to be your role model doing your lesson, playing for your exam or just when you are practising.
>
> Enjoy feeling their confidence and the way they play your music.
>
> You can take them with you everywhere you go. It doesn't do any harm to pretend, but it will give you extra self-assurance.

Chapter 20

In the Zone

To be 'in the zone' is the ultimate in mental preparation. It doesn't matter what has just happened, or what might happen. Only what you are playing *now* counts.

The mind is in a state of such complete absorption that there is no vestige of self-awareness. The zone, or mindfulness, is where one is totally aware in any situation and so is able to respond appropriately. The mind is not so much settled on any one thing, but aware of your whole being. You use your hands where they are needed, you use your legs or your eyes where they are needed and no time or energy will go to waste.

All this sounds daunting. What it boils down to is aiming to take the focus away from 'trying' too hard, and letting your focus of attention be more rounded. You need to listen to the music you are making, and not be absorbed in the actual task of making it happen.

Being 'in the zone' means to:

- **Be in charge:**

As you practise, notice where you feel physically secure and mentally clear, connected to and comfortable with the music.

- **Concentrate on making your playing feel and sound enjoyable for you:**

When you enjoy your music, the audience or examiner will pick up those vibes and enjoy it too.

- **Play from your hara point:**

This is found just below your tummy button and about halfway between your back and your front. It is the point at which your body is fully balanced. To play from deep down here means that your body is controlled and centred, you are in control of your muscles and are far away from any distracting chatter from the critics in your head. You can make beautiful music with warmth and love from the depths of your inner self.

- **Be aware:**

If you slip up, go back and tackle the section thoroughly. Listen to your fears, for they are telling you what is still not secure.

Get to know what you *can* do by doing *too much*.
Rather than getting the notes right try:

- To deliberately make mistakes.
- To deliberately intensify your nerves.
- To play too fast or too slow.
- To experiment, e.g. play a sad piece cheerfully or a happy piece sadly.

- **Visualise the situation:**

See yourself playing wonderfully but also see the examiner and how she/he is enjoying your playing.

- **Practise playing in a safe environment:**

Play to a group of friends or family. At the end of your performance they have to say something positive about what you did. You also have to say something that you were pleased with.

- **Have a chat with your inner critic:**

This can be done by having two chairs, or two cushions, placed opposite one another. Sit in one and from there talk to the other chair where your inner critic is. You can ask it such questions as, "why do you expect me to be perfect all the time?" Or "you'll give me such a hard time if I mess up on the day, won't you?" Then swap chairs and you become the inner critic and you can reply to yourself, "You know you can do that page perfectly but I'll be happy if you just do your best!"

While you are playing your exam piece, listen to:

- **The emotions in the music.** Listen out for any, or all of the human emotions of happiness, sadness, anger, and fear. Some music has little obvious emotional state, the richness of the music being in the musical argument. Other music has clear emotions and, to make sense of them, the musician needs to be attentive and respond with the same emotion.

- **The rhythm in the music.** In popular and jazz music you need to let the rhythms flow in a natural way, whereas in classical music, dance rhythms underlie many compositions but may need a more taut shape built round a basic pulse.

- **The sound and dynamics of the music.** Also listen to the balance between either different instruments, if you are an instrumentalist playing with a piano accompaniment for example, or between the hands for a pianist.

- **The meaning of the music.** Music may have words, which makes it easier to find the clues that explain the emotions in the music, but if not there is always some sort of structure with suspense and resolution, or a series of arguments with phrases that question, elaborate, digress, modify or answer.

To be 'in the zone' you need to take your focus away from what may be inhibiting your performance and place it on what is enhancing it.

Put it another way: stop listening to the inner critic and listen to the music you are making instead.

"What is 'being in the zone' like?"

At the peak of tremendous and victorious effort, when the blood is pounding through your head, all suddenly becomes quiet within you.

Everything seems clearer and whiter than before. At that moment you have the conviction that you have all the power in the world, that you are capable of anything and that you have wings.

When you are in 'the zone', you have switched from a training mode to a trusting one. You are not fighting yourself; you're not afraid of anything; you're living in the moment in a special time and place.

The harder you try to get into the zone, however, the further away you will get. The zone is your reward for all your hard work and preparation. Just go with the flow and enjoy the moment. Don't try to make something happen; just trust your practice and hard work and let the music just flow from your fingers.

> "Our control is best when we are least aware of it."
> Yehudi Menuhin, famous violinist.

Athletes get themselves into the zone where they can see themselves performing at their best. Here is a short technique to help you to take care over these troublesome areas and to get you into the performing zone. It is called the slo-mo-action-replay.

The Slo-Mo-Action-Replay:

For this practice session you are just going to imagine that you have already done your performance and that it went fantastically well. What did you do especially well? Was it the dynamics, or did that line of semiquavers flow along fluently and clearly? Tell yourself the aspects of this performance you were particularly pleased with.

Now sit quietly and comfortably, in a place where you will not be disturbed for about ten minutes and do the exercise on the next page:

Close your eyes if you want to and watch a film of yourself playing superbly, with flow and fluency.

Take your time.

You can watch yourself play with freedom and passion. You can re-run and change your movie to build up a better picture of yourself. See yourself playing those *staccati* clearly and crisply, but if you don't see this, then re-run the movie and imagine it again with really good notes this time.

Run through the movie again and hear your flowing *legato* lines.

Do it all slowly, editing the movie and the soundtrack until it is perfect so that, at every stage, you make yourself feel confident and delightfully in control. See the end of the concert, with the audience clapping and cheering, and sense that wonderful feeling inside you of success and confidence.

Once you are happy with your movie you are going to run it again, slowly, enjoying every moment of your total performance, really enjoying every note and every positive feeling.

Make everything vivid, bright and colourful.

When you have finished your movie, gently come back to the room and just take pleasure in the lovely feelings you have experienced.

These are not dreams. They are not times when you sit there in your chair and say, "If only…" These are times when you build up your strong mental image of what is possible, of what you can do well, and what you can expect to do.

Music is not only what you play; it is also what you hear in your head. It can be as real to you before it is played as the actual work can be. Your maximum possible performance range is partly determined by your capacity to deal with this potential richness and reproduce it when you need it in a musical event. So, you can see, it is really worth your while taking the time to do these mental exercises.

It also has another effect in that it can help you if you are feeling low, dispirited and lacking self-assurance.

Confidence is knowing it will be all right on the night.

Sit down and get comfortable and try this easy idea on the next page to calm yourself if you are feeling nervous:

There are two slightly raised bumps on your forehead about 2–3 centimetres above the eyes on an adult, known as the frontal eminences. Lightly place the pads of your fingers of one hand over these eminences, gently stretching the skin. You may feel a slight pulse here. You may notice that the pulse from one bump is not the same as the other bump, but that is quite normal, especially if you are nervous or worried.

In your mind, go over the situation that is worrying you. It might be something that has already happened, or something coming in the future. Relive it or pretend it in all the detail you can, making all the images you see in your mind as clear and vivid as you can. Think of it as if you are making a video diary of the event.

Think hard about all the negative things that you can, but don't worry if you can't remember all the details.

Play the video again, and once more.

Find a statement that is positive and sums up what you really want.

Say your statement (e.g. "I will play in a calm way") or find a trigger word (such as "calm" or "control") and roll your eyes in a very slow, wide circle first in one direction and then back in the other.

Take your fingers off now.

You should be feeling that the event is less important, or a bit foggy, or disappeared all together. You may find that you yawn, sigh or simply take a deep breath. This shows that you have succeeded in changing how you feel about the event. This might have taken 20 seconds, or ten minutes - it doesn't matter how long it takes.

Chapter 21

Physical Preparation for Performance

In order to feel secure when you are performing you will need all your aural, kinaesthetic (physical) and intellectual/visual (mental) skills. You need to know the *sound* of every note you play, whether it is in the melody or in the harmony, the *feel* of every note you play and the *look* of every note required both on the page and on the instrument.

You need to make certain that your body is comfortable. Your muscles will resist learning anything that is uncomfortable because they know that this might result in injury.

You need to keep concentrating so you keep a clear mental image of your piece and listen carefully to how you are playing it.

Practise, using all your skills:

- Slowly, using a speed at which you don't make mistakes, rhythmically, firmly and with an inner feeling of warmth.
- Hands separately with and without sound.
- Hands together with and without sound.
- Fingering and saying the note names.
- Fingering and counting out loud.
- Use distorted rhythms.
- Analyse the written music to understand the overall shape, form, themes, patterns etc.

- Practise from memory, looking at the instrument being aware of the keys and fingering patterns. Do this task hands separately if possible, even on a wind instrument. (We hardly ever think about what each hand does when we have to use both hands to produce the fingering for one note. Do you know what your right hand does separately from your left when playing, for example, an upper D or F?)
- Divide the music into musically appropriate sections and make sure you can pick the music up from any of these places. Practise these **pick-up points** hands separately and together, with or without sound.
- Visualise playing the notes away from the instrument, section by section, hands together and separately, inwardly hearing the sound and imagine feeling the sensations of playing through your fingers.

"What if I mess up?"

There are two answers to this very natural fear.

The first one is to practise thoroughly so that you don't mess up, but that is really not very helpful, is it? Being a human being, and being under pressure due to the up-and-coming concert or exam, you are very likely to do something unexpected. If you have worked diligently through *Let's Practise,* you have certainly eliminated many of the possible danger areas.

The second answer is to consider the 'what if...?' scenario. What if you mess up? What if you forget where you are in the music? What if someone coughs loudly and puts you off?

You need to accept that you may have glitches in your playing; however, you need a plan in place should they arise. Most pupils, if they go wrong, will either start again, flap around trying to find the right notes, or run out of the room altogether.

We are going to try and **mask** the mistake so that the listener doesn't realise that there was even an error at all. This takes practice.

You are going to find some landmark places in your music that are called **pick-up points**. These are bars or notes in the music where you feel really confident about what the music is doing, and where you know that you could start from if things go wrong.

Pick-Up Points:

> You need to find some 'pick-up' points. It probably is a good idea to have them every four bars, or at the beginning of the phrases or half phrases. If this seems too many, then have points every couple of lines or so.
>
> Practise these pick-up points so that you know them well, including fingering and dynamics. These are important places, so get to know them well by playing them at least ten times a day.
>
> To make them useful, in the next practices, if you make a mistake don't redo that section, jump on to your nearest pick-up point.
>
> To make any jump from a mistake to a pick-up point successful you could practise playing *something* whilst you make the join. You could play repeated notes, or several slow ones – anything as you make your way to the nearest pick-up place. But keep a straight face, and don't give the game away that you have just gone wrong!
>
> Now you need to practise, hoping to make a mistake so that you can use your new skill.

OK! It may not be perfect, but it is a lot more musical than just stopping or going back to the beginning.

"But if I jump from one place to another, won't there be a gap in the music?"

There is a danger that you will have a gap where you jump from one pick-up point to the next, so a more musical way of covering up the hole where the notes should have been is to **invent** something to go into the space.

Invent:

> Rather than just leaping on to the next pick-up point, play anything; a single note will do. Play a C or a D. Play it beautifully and with passion and keep playing it while you find your next pick-up point.
>
> If you feel more inventive, you could try playing a scale or an arpeggio, or simply a few random notes, preferably in the key of the piece you are playing.

I know that this might seem a bit strange, but you will surprised to hear that most people will not even notice that you had messed up when you did your inventing. They may say it sounded a bit odd, but you can just smile and think to yourself, "you have no idea!"

This trick will work as long as you keep a **straight face**. If you pull a face, go as red as a beetroot or sigh, you will have given the game away. The audience will guess that something must be wrong, indeed you may as well have stopped and shouted out that you have gone wrong. Don't give them the chance to spot your mistake. You may not fool everyone, but if you pull a face, you will fool no one.

Don't let anxiety prevent you from doing your best. You can attack your fears about performing in front of others by using some energy tapping techniques. These sound a bit quirky, but, as people who have used *Mind Over Matter* have discovered, these strange and under-used methods can revolutionise your anxiety levels. It is based on the ancient Chinese art of acupuncture, but instead of using needles to energise your body, this technique uses a gentle and simple method of tapping two fingers on specific points on your body. (This tapping procedure is taken from *Energy Tapping* by Gallo and Vincenzi, 2000.) It would be worth reading this through before you start because at first glance it looks a little complicated.

Energy tapping:

1. Turn your hand so you can see the palm of your hand, find the palm crease that is closest to your fingers and notice where

the crease crosses the edge of the hand closest to the little finger.

2. Tap this spot gently with two fingers of the other hand while saying three times, "I deeply accept myself even though I am afraid that the examiner will not like my playing."

3. Now, if you had to choose how anxious you feel on a scale of 1 to 10 (with 1 meaning that you don't really feel anxious and 10 being that you feel ready to run and hide), decide what score you would give it.

4. Tap very gently (so that you can only just feel it) with two fingers of one hand, five times each, on each of these points and in this order:

- Under your eye - under the centre of your eye on the tip of the bone.
- Under your arm - six centimetres under your armpit.
- Under your collarbone - two or three centimetres under your collarbone near your throat.

Rate your anxiety again - a number should just pop into your mind.

If there is no change, try the list again.

If you feel less worried, then go on and do the Brain Balancer.

Brain Balancer:

- Tap repeatedly on the back of your hand between the little finger and ring finger knuckles at the base of the knuckle.
- Roll your eyes once round clockwise.
- Roll your eyes once round anti-clockwise.
- Hum *Happy Birthday* to yourself.
- Count to five out loud.
- Hum *Happy Birthday* again.

Repeat steps 1 – 4 of the Energy Tapping sequence again.

If your anxiety level has now dropped to 2, 1 or 0 then tap the back of your hand again, but this time move your eyes from down to up and down again without moving your head.

Amazing, isn't it?

There is another way you can do the above technique but you need to have done the tapping example first. This can be used as a short cut method if you begin to feel anxious. Instead of tapping, you use two fingers to place mild pressure:

- on the side of your hand - and say, "I accept myself even if I mess this bit up."
- under your nose - and say, "I can do this section."

Whilst relaxation and rest are often recommended before a big event, if you are feeling too full of energy, then use the adrenalin from your 'fight or flight' response to release tension. Walk about or run up and down stairs if it helps to use up excess energy and calm you down.

Chapter 22

Preparing for the Big Day

The problem for students doing their exam or concert is starting off with those first few notes. You have arrived in the exam room or on the stage and are prepared to begin your pieces. Suddenly you are there, about to actually perform. This is it! The moment of truth! You have spent weeks and weeks working towards this big day. This is when you will find out what the acoustics are like and how the piano feels. Now you will need to establish the tempo, silence any inner critic, and, at the same time, remember what the notes are, where your hands go, what the dynamics are and what the style is.

Unfortunately, all of this occurs at the time when you are probably feeling most anxious, and the first few moments can be overpowering. This might result in you feeling your way through the first few bars, just hoping that all will settle down after the first lines of music.

Of course, you expect that all will be well after a couple of minutes, but then, what happens if it doesn't? There is nothing worse, after a bad start, than finding that you are still lurching from one disaster to another. Nerves make you feel even more tense, so your fingers are too stiff, or your breathing gets worse and worse, and you feel the whole thing falling away from you.

So, it is essential that you practise starting your performance.

Practising the start:

What will you need to think about before you play that very first note? What about the opening phrase or two? Make a list of things you will have to consider. It might look like this:

- What are my first notes?
- How fast does it to go?
- What dynamic level do I need?
- What articulation will I use?
- What is my posture like?

Now you have a list, you are going to play just those opening bars, but only focussing on one issue at a time. You can experience, with those opening bars, the successful delivery of each of these items. You are going to imagine that this is the big day and that you are just about to go on stage or enter the exam room.

You choose just one element that you want to have good control over, such as the tempo.

Leave the room, taking your instrument with you. Now, walk back into the room as if you were going to begin your concert or exam. Imagine that your examiner is sitting at a table in the room. Greet your imaginary examiner politely and with a smile. Then pause and consider carefully the tempo you need to go at and then play just a few bars of the beginning of your first piece. Since you are only focussing on the start, there is no need to do much of the piece, but stop instead and reflect on what you have just done. Were you successful at establishing the correct tempo?

If you were pleased with what you did, then keep practising the start, just as you have done – walking in to the room, greeting your examiner and playing the entry. Repeat this process several times in fifteen minutes.

It is not just a dream, or something you can't control, but, as you can see, you can practise a confident start to your exam or concert. You will have done the start of your piece more times and prepared it better than if you just left it to chance.

Repeat the whole process again with another element you would like to control until you have worked through all the items that you were concerned about.

Regrettably, we need to do more than one thing at a time, so now it is time to combine a couple of elements. Each time you play your opening bars, consider carefully whether this is the effect you wanted. If not, then think about what needs to happen and try again with your new idea. By the end of the session, you should have combined all of the items on your list and enjoyed making a successful start.

- Now you have formed a clear idea of how your music actually begins, and this is good in itself.
- You also have learnt how your start should go so that you can control the beginning.
- You will be able to make a confident entry into the exam room, and have an air of authority from the very first step.

So much hangs on your state of mind, though, when you are in the spotlight. No matter how well you have prepared yourself, if your confidence is low and you expect disaster, then disaster is almost bound to happen. If, however, you exude confidence, then you will find that you can cope with mistakes and still keep going.

How are you going to gain this confidence, even in the midst of all the anxiety of these opening minutes? One way is to make a list of all the enjoyable moments in your music.

1. List all the things you love playing in your pieces:

Make a list of all the phrases, bars, sections, *crescendos*, *rallentandos* and other ideas that you really enjoy or you know you play really well. Rather than focussing on the problem bits and worrying about disasters, you are going to think about all the parts of your music you enjoy doing. So, even if you have wrong notes, they will be wrong notes filled with wonderful dynamics or the quavers will be extremely *legato*, even if they are not correct. These are areas in the music that you can count on to go well. Write a list of these successful places and even mark them in your music so you can see them coming up during your performance and look forward to them.

The second way you can prepare your mind to feel confident is to visualise the event in your imagination. This is a very powerful tool as the mind can be influenced positively by thinking and imagining.

2.   Visualise:

Now, visualise playing this piece with these ideas in mind.

Find a quiet place where you can sit uninterrupted for a few minutes.

Close your eyes and get really comfortable.

What you are going to do now is imagine playing through your piece only focussing on the sections, bars, or dynamics that you can guarantee you can play well and that you enjoy playing.

For instance, if you love the beginning melody and you enjoy the gentle *crescendo*, then play this bit in your mind, smile as you play it, and enjoy the feeling of it deep within you.

Then, skip forward, without hearing the next bit in your mind if it is a weak area; leap on to the next wonderful section and play that, smiling as you do it and enjoying the feeling of playing it so well.

Leap on again and again, leaving out any poor bits, only hearing in your mind the best elements.

When you have successfully played this piece in your mind, stay with the picture in your mind: think of your feelings of pleasure, enjoyment and satisfaction for a few more moments, and then slowly and gently come back to a sense of your surroundings and open your eyes.

If you still have problem areas this close to the performance it is not too late to still be targeting them. You need to throw everything you have at learning the tricky bits. You may have to devote extra practice time to these bits, since you cannot stop work on your preparation of the good parts and working on the beginning of your piece.

Chapter 23

Three Weeks To Go

In the final three weeks prior to your performance you need to pay careful attention to how you practise. You need to shift into a very positive mental attitude. Your music has been sped up, memorised and polished, and now the attention turns to *you*, the student.

1. Be prepared: the mock exam.

Borrow a member of your family to be the examiner; it doesn't matter if they know anything about music or not. However, they can do all the things that a real examiner will do. So, once the 'examiner' asks to you to sit down (or tune up), you are in an exam situation.

You will need to give them a list of all your scales, a piece of sight-reading, a piece of paper for writing a report and a pencil to write down the score. You might give them a timer too, so that they have to use their time well.

Your 'examiner' puts the timer on for ten minutes and then is allowed to start with anything she/he likes: pieces, scales or sight-reading. Whoever is examining you, whether you are playing your pieces or scales, you need to play through them at one go, getting them right the first time, just as you would in the real exam.

The difference between this and the real thing (apart from the obvious, that you won't be performing at home, and you won't have a family member pretending to examine you!) will be that the pretend 'examiner' can do things in any order, and ask for them as many times as they like. They could ask you for D major in the left hand, and get you to play your second piece twice! They might even stop you halfway through some of your pieces. You will be surprised at how unsettling this sort of test can be. You might feel quite nervous and get anxious.

That is precisely the idea. By the time your exam comes, you will be almost unruffled by the real thing.

After each mock exam, you will make your own list of things that you messed up, and things that didn't work. The advantage of doing this sort of exam is that, whereas in a real test you can't go back and do it again, with this one you can have as many goes as you like. You can go and do some work on the bits you felt unhappy with before your next mock exam.

The idea is to find out all the sections, bars, scales and fingering that don't yet stand up to pressure and help you build up your stamina for having to concentrate (and stand if necessary) for the duration of the exam. You get a chance to work on the bits that might otherwise have let you down on the day.

You can do as many mock tests as you like, but try to do at least one a week before the exam or concert.

To have a second chance is better than having no chance at all.

2.   Be prepared: The sibling test.

The next unpleasant idea is to have someone like your little sister in the room with you as you prepare for the exam.

You are going to go through your pieces as if you were playing for an exam or concert, so you are going to play straight through your pieces and scales, BUT while you are doing this, your sister is going to try to distract you. She can bang a table, clap her hands, stamp her feet, rattle some keys, poke you if you make a mistake, throw socks at you, look up the end of your flute, …anything to try to put you off. If you get through this test without either laughing your head off or crashing out, then WELL DONE!

Is this too straightforward? Try the next game.

3.   The 'I wonder if' game.

I wonder if I can….

- Play whilst raising one eyebrow and then the other while I play?
- Wiggle my hips?
- Twitch my nose?
- Play with the lights off?
- Run on the spot for five minutes and then perform my piece while I'm out of breath?
- Play the piece with my eyes shut?
- Hold a bag of frozen peas for two minutes and then play my music with ice-cold hands?
- Say the alphabet forwards as I play?
- Say the alphabet backwards as I play?
- Make up lyrics to the main melody while I am playing? Can I make those lyrics rhyme?
- Hum my piece through in my head, stop at random and play from there?

When you play in the exam room or the concert hall there are bound to be things that happen that surprise you or are beyond your control. You cannot predict what might happen, but compared with what you have put up with in your practice sessions it will seem like nothing. You don't want to have these sessions too often, but if you can get through them, you will cope with anything. All you will need to do for the concert or the exam is just to play your pieces. No tricks, no distractions, no challenges, just play. How easy will that seem?

4. Record Yourself.

With three weeks to go you are going to record your whole performance.

This practice session is going to be less like your normal way of working and more like the actual performance. It will be a complete run through of everything, with no stops, no repeating of bits that went wrong, proper tempo, and if done properly, will put a little edge on the performance that will show you how you are reacting to working under pressure.

This first run-through rehearsal will allow you to play and prepare in privacy, but it is not so much the performance, but what you will *hear* on the recording that is going to be important.

Prepare your music and switch on your recorder. You will even start by walking on to your 'stage', and bow to your audience or smile and make eye-contact with your examiner just as you will on the day. Tune up, as you will do on the day. Then start to play your first piece, and go on through all your pieces until you have finished …then stop. Pick up your pieces and leave your stage. Switch off your recorder.

Don't worry about how satisfied you were with the final result. This practice session was not about how well you played, but about *what you are going to do next*. You are going to **listen** to your recording of yourself playing.

5. Listen Really Carefully.

Now you have to listen really carefully to what you produced in your rehearsal. You need to identify the things that worked better than you expected. Make a note of it because you need to think through why it worked better. Did you *crescendo* well, or do more tonguing? You are going to do it that way for every future play-through.

Did those tricky bits re-appear?

You probably have worked hard on those awkward bits and broken them down and repaired them too, the bits where the thought goes through your head, "Oh no, here is the bit I hate." Well, I am afraid to say that you need to go back over them but change your practice scheme. Choose some other tools to help you sort out these bits again such as some of the games in the Quality not Quantity chapter.

Did other bits go wrong?

These sections often come as a surprise to us. We have worked on the tricky bars and now discover it is the bits that we didn't feel we needed to attend to so much that go awry.

The thing is, is this the only time this bit has gone wrong? If it is then don't worry about it, but think through why it might have gone wrong in this playing. Did you actually take that bit at a different speed from the one you usually choose? Was there a moment of doubt that crept into your mind just as you got to this bit? Was there some sloppy fingering just beforehand that caused your hand to end up in the wrong place? Well, all of those you can fix by listening to your performance and noting and practising what you have discovered.

Two other issues may also have shown up:

- Did you discover that, by putting pressure on your performance by recording it, you didn't in fact know that piece as well as you thought you did? Go back to all those ideas in Part 1 and do the **Downfall** game, or **In the Pots**.

- You have listened really carefully to your playing and analysed it well. This is a good exercise in itself, for what we hear back is not always what we think we are doing. It has been also useful for you to hear what has worked and what hasn't.

Don't be tempted to re-run your pieces now, although you can start work on some bits that need sorting out. After all, we can all get our pieces correct if we continue to play them twenty or thirty times, but the object of the exercise was to see how the pieces stood up under pressure. Therefore don't do any more re-runs today, although you can try again tomorrow or when you feel you have done some quality work on your music.

Any tricky bits that re-appeared have to be addressed now, before it is too late. If not, you will only start to feel anxious about them and begin to feel fearful of the event because you will have thoughts running through your mind, such as "what if it goes wrong, and I mess up?" instead of being focussed and getting into the performing zone.

You will have to throw every trick of the trade that you know at this problem. You will have to stick at it and give up your time to get the tiger tamed. Bite the bullet and set to work, and work and work until you have achieved a tame tiger. It is the only way you will ever gain confidence and freedom to play your piece well.

Chapter 24

Two Weeks To Go

Record your pieces:

You can keep recording your pieces during this coming week, but with only two weeks to go before the concert or exam you need to play to another person - a friend or a parent. Once again, it is a once-only situation, and once again, you will need to listen carefully to your playing and comment critically as you did on your own recording now you have an audience.

Dress Rehearsal:

If you can find people to play to, do this type of dress rehearsal as many times as you feel you need to before the day, although many teachers will advise you not to play in this way forty-eight hours before the event. This is partly because they worry that, if you make slips in these last few hours you might not have enough time to fix them properly and then have areas for your inner voice to give you a hard time about when you approach weak areas in your music during the concert.

Penalty shoot-out:

Ideally, you should try this every day (but only once a day) prior to your exam or concert. It is nasty, but you will thank yourself for it after the event. You do this as the last item of your practice session.

You get one shot at goal, which is to play your piece through from beginning to end without any mistakes. If it is a long piece then you can do just a big section of it. You have to play it through perfectly. You will have to do this in two weeks' time after all.

If nothing goes wrong then you can stop and finish your practice there.

If you miss the goal, then you have to do twenty minutes more practice.

Yes, I said it was nasty! You need to start work immediately on the very bit that let you down and work on it for twenty minutes. Better luck tomorrow!

Some pupils find this quite stressful, but it does help them find the weak bits of their pieces and get them fixed before the concert or exam. It might make you feel quite nervous or anxious about the piece, but it is better to practise like this than discover it on the day.

Visiting the venue:

It might be an idea to ask if you can visit the venue where you will be performing, if it is a place you have not been to before. It would be good if you could play your instrument there to get a feel for the acoustics and see how the room is set up.

This will help you to visualise yourself playing there, with panache, vigour and emotion.

Chapter 25

Just Before the Performance

Success comes from the peace of mind of knowing that you have tried your very best. You have practised well, done some mock exams and prepared yourself emotionally, mentally and physically.

Centring yourself:

Sit comfortably with a straight back and your feet firmly on the floor. Imagine that you are slightly above your own head and want to connect fully with your *hara* point and thus connect with your musical expression. Often, when we are anxious, we are too 'high' up in the body: we speak fast and with a higher-pitched voice than we would normally use; we breathe more rapidly and move quickly.

Count backwards from ten to one and then imagine that a golden cloud is passing over the top of your head, down behind your eyes, nose, mouth, down your windpipe, collarbones, chest, tummy, and down to your *hara* point. Stay there and enjoy the feeling of your emotions and the balance of that and your mental awareness.

Here are some tips for the morning of your concert or exam:

- Breathe deeply and rhythmically from the diaphragm.
- Chew some gum. You don't want anything sweet in case your mouth gets sticky and dry, but you need to encourage your mouth to make saliva as part of your control over any anxieties you may be feeling.
- Move, because your body needs to use its muscles, so jog gently, touch your toes, do some Brain Gym exercises like cross-crawl to flex your muscles.
- Make sure your hands are neither too hot nor too cold: immerse them in the appropriate temperature water.
- If you are feeling nervous then tell yourself or someone else. This helps you to get in touch with yourself and enables you to centre yourself even in your nervousness.
- Visualise yourself playing the opening of your pieces, playing with warmth, enjoyment and with a wonderful tone.
- Remember the points from your 'starting off' practice.
- Centre yourself and play from your *hara* point. (See the chapter on In The Zone.)

Chapter 26

During a Performance

When the lights go on, it's show time. Be prepared in mind, body and spirit to do battle. Even so, there will be times during the performance that things just don't go quite as planned.

Here are some ideas that you can take with you into that exam room or concert platform:

1. Pieces of music are not made up of just tricky bits. There are parts of the music that you may actually **enjoy** playing. It is important to know where these parts are in your music, and then you can look forward to playing them and showing off that you can do these bits with confidence.

2. One of the most important things to take with you is **love**. Knowing that you love what you are doing, loving the music, knowing how lucky you are to be able to play at all, is such a strong and basic ingredient for success.

3. **Laughter** is also a very important factor in music making. Don't let the exam situation kill your sense of fun. Having fun, even in the midst of disaster, is a good way of calming yourself. You need to think of something silly while you are playing, like **frogs** or **holidays**.

Frogs or holidays:

This seems a peculiar idea, but it works and it goes like this:

You are playing along, and you make a tiny mistake. A mere nothing, but it is a bit disturbing and it affects your confidence a bit. Now you are a fraction less confident, and therefore a fraction more likely to make another mistake.

A few bars later and there goes another little glitch, and a few bars later you make another small slip. It keeps on going like this.

The more you think about it, the worse things will get. So you must get out of this loop of mistakes. It would be good if you could get your inner carer to step in and help. She/he does – and into your mind pop silly ideas, like frogs, or holidays. Excuse me? You have been taught to concentrate and focus on the notes and here come some jumping frogs? You are not to let your mind wander and here you are thinking about your holiday!

The reason why this appears to work is that, when you start thinking of odd ideas, it is as if part of your mind is released to get on with the job of playing while your thoughts are distracted onto frogs or holidays.

It really doesn't matter what you think of, the idea is to distract yourself and stop thinking about the mistakes. In this way you may divert yourself from making a mess-up.

Chapter 27

Parents

A large amount of research shows that musical ability runs in families and is more prevalent when both biological parents and grandparents are musical. Not all the members of such families need to be musicians themselves but several are likely to have potential musical ability: being able to sing in tune, remember melodies easily, hear musical intervals and rhythms and understand the notes in harmonies.

Despite the favourable influence of family background, studies show that several highly talented musicians have come from humble homes where there is little musical activity, and that there is up to twenty-five percent chance that a child will be musical even if neither parent is apparently so. It is equally true that a number of children from musical families show little musical motivation or talent.

Is musical ability due to nature or nurture? It is difficult to determine whether genes or having a musical upbringing decide musical ability because the home will already have played a role by the time musical ability is apparent. Thus, it may be partly an innate talent, but is a skill that is enhanced by a favourable environment.

Early rewards:

One of the most important factors in the making of future musicians is the amount of reward given for signs of musical promise. In a home where there are musical instruments a child may be encouraged to play them from an early age and early efforts, whether they are banging on a drum or strumming a guitar, are met with applause.

Young children associate clapping and applause with being clever; thus, a very early link is made between performing and receiving love and attention from family members. Other positive associations with love and closeness come from listening to music, as when a child sits on a parent's knee while she/he plays the piano, or when parents sing to their child.

These early associations may be pleasurable and are like magic to a young child's imagination. Music is like an enchanted world of sound, rhythm and feelings. Creating it makes good things happen, just like fairies and mystical spells cause good things to happen in stories. Music brings love, closeness, excitement, rewards, applause and all sorts of other positive things. So, music is firmly fixed in the emotions as a good thing. Later, the child's recognisable attempts to imitate tunes are further rewarded, and when there are attempts at composition these too get added to the list of 'good things'.

Children of three or under are unlikely to play musical instruments but specialist classes, where they can enjoy musical activities, would be of enormous benefit. Parents need to be aware, though, of their comments to the random banging on the piano or a saucepan lid. If you say, "That was interesting, what was it supposed to be?" rather than, "Stop that awful noise!" then you will be encouraging your child's musical imagination. Singing with your child, even if you are not very good at it, will really help your child to develop musically. Children older than three could start Kodaly or Dalcroze classes with their parents, but it is usually between six and nine when most children begin the serious business of learning an instrument.

So one of the roles of a parent is to encourage their children. However, one of the problems that they face is how to help you, the student.

They don't need to be able to play an instrument themselves in order to help you on your way to becoming a musician.

Parents need to:

Show interest:

Parents need to be interested in what you are doing. Talk to them about your music. Can you show your parents how to put your flute together or how you get your lowest note on your saxophone? Do they know how you are feeling as you wait for your exam? Do they know where your tricky bits are and how you are trying to fix them?

Give support:

Parents need to support your learning by doing the checkpoints with you and keeping an eye on your Big Day deadline chart. (See the chapter on Organising Your Time.) They are needed for playing the games like Noughts and Crosses, or the Penalty Shoot-Out. They need to understand what and how you are practising for the week so that they are in a position to help and encourage you. Their role is to help you to get over problems, for example, if you fall behind in your practice schedule by helping you plan how you are going to catch up, and not to nag about the fact that you have missed a deadline.

Give encouragement:

Parents can take you to hear music and to help you to enjoy being a musician. They can help develop your love for the hobby you have chosen, and perhaps to see you on your way to Music College and a musical career.

Just be there for you:

Sometimes parents are best when they are just there in the background, letting you have room to develop and work on your own. The very fact that they have probably read this book with you and taken on board some of the ideas is almost sufficient to encourage and enthuse you in this most amazing of life skills, that of making music.

Conclusion

Well done!

Even if you have taken only a fraction of the ideas in this book you will have a clearer idea of how to practise and prepare for performance. You will be mentally stronger, emotionally richer and physically better prepared for your music making.

Remember to practise thoughtfully and carefully, listening to yourself and being prepared to give some time to correct any mistakes. Stay focussed on your task, but work in a relaxed way, breathing well, and enjoying the sounds and atmospheres that you are making.

Take note of the chapters on preparing for performance and you will feel more in control of the situation when you are playing in public, and you may even enjoy the experience!

Good and happy playing,

Susan Whykes

Index of Games

Appendix

Weekly Planner

Weekly Planner plus Rewards Day

Deadline Planner

Weekly Planner

Date			Lesson Time			
	Piece 1	Piece 2	Piece 3	Scales	Aural	Theory
	Tools:	Tools:	Tools:			
Day 1						
Day 2						
Day 3						
Day 4						
Day 5						
Day 6						
Day 7						
Comments						

Weekly Planner Plus Rewards Day

Date			Lesson Time			
	Piece 1	Piece 2	Piece 3	Scales	Aural	Theory
	Tools:	Tools:	Tools:			
Day 1						
Day 2						
Day 3 DAY OFF	Must be able to:			Must be able to:		
Day 4						
Day 5						
Day 6 DAY OFF	Must be able to:			Must be able to:		
Day 7						
Comments						

Deadline Planner

Date		
Date	1 week from now must be able to play:	
	2 weeks from now must be able to play:	
	3 weeks from now must be able to play:	
	4 weeks from now must be able to play:	
	5 weeks from now must be able to play:	
	6 weeks from now must be able to play:	
	7 weeks from now must be able to play:	
	8 weeks from now:	All pieces memorised All scales memorised
	9 weeks from now:	Scales test
	10 weeks from now:	Record all pieces
	11 weeks from now:	Mock performance
	12 weeks from now:	BIG DAY!

Bibliography:

Bull, S.J. (1995); *Sport Psychology – A Self-Help Guide;* The Crowood Press Ltd. Ramsbury, Malborough, Wiltshire SN8 2HR.

Charles, R. (2000); *Your Mind's Eye: How to Heal Yourself and Release Your Potential Through Creative Visualisation;* Piatkus Books. Little Brown Book Group, 100 Victoria Embankment, London EC4Y 0DY.

Dennison, P.E. and Dennison, G.E. (1989); *Brain Gym;* Edu-Kinesthetics, Inc. Ventura, California.

Edwards, A. (1994); *The Secrets of Musical Confidence*; HarperCollins Publishers. 77-85 Fulham Palace Road, Hammersmith, London W6 8JB.

Gallo, F.P. and Vincenzi, H. (2000); *Energy Tapping*; New Harbinger Publications, Inc. 5674 Shattuck Ave, Oakland, CA 94609.

Green, B. and Gallwey, W.T. (1987); *The Inner Game of Music*; Pan Books. Macmillan General Books, 25 Eccleston Place, London, SW1W 9NF.

Harris, P. and Crozier, R. (2001); *The Music Teacher's Companion*; ABRSM Publishing. 24 Portland Place, London, W1B 1LU.

Johnston, P. (2007); *The Practice Revolution;* PracticeSpot Press. 52 Pethebridge Street, Pearce, ACT 2607, Australia.

Mack, G. and Casstevens, D. (2001); *Mind Gym*; McGraw-Hill, 2 Pewnn Plaza, New York, NY 10121-2298.

Mackworth-Young, L. (2000); *Tuning In*; MMM Publications. The Houghton Centre for the Arts, Houghton-on-the-Hill, South Pickenham, Swaffham, Norfolk, PE37 8DP.

Taylor, C. (1982); *These Music Exams;* The Associated Board of the Royal Schools of Music, 24 Portland Place, London, W1B 1LU.

Whykes, S. (2007); *Mind Over Matter*; AuthorHouse UK Ltd, 500 Avebury Boulevard, Central Milton Keynes, MK9 2BE.